WHISTLER'S WALK

WHISTLER'S WALK

THE APPALACHIAN TRAIL IN 142 DAYS

WILLIAM MONK

Palmetto Publishing Group
Charleston, SC

Whistler's Walk
Copyright © 2018 by William Monk
All rights reserved

First Edition

Printed in the United States

ISBN-13: 978-1-64111-095-2
ISBN-10: 1-64111-095-3

The woods are lovely, dark and deep,
But I have promises to keep,
And miles to go before I sleep,
And miles to go before I
sleep.

—Robert Frost, "Stopping by Woods on a
Snowy Evening"

FOREWORD

Whistler's entertaining and compelling journey, as chronicled in the coming pages, started about twenty-two years ago when we were living briefly in northern Georgia. Whistler is my dad, and when I was in middle school, we took advantage of our proximity to the Appalachian Trail to hike a little bit one summer with some of his friends, one of whom was an experienced outdoorsman who handled most of the details for us. We had a great time, and decided that the next summer, my dad and I would take a week and hike a section, just the two of us.

When Annie (my mom) and Brian (my brother, and Whistler's younger son) dropped us off that second year, we said our goodbyes at the bottom of the mountain, which was where we'd been picked up the year before. We started to walk uphill, and we were carrying too much weight in our packs without having done enough physical conditioning—a seriously stupid amount of weight. For example, we had frozen hamburger for stroganoff that first night, and a thermos of ice-cold milk for chocolate pudding. A few hundred yards up the mountain, we were sucking wind and wondering (honestly) if we should call Annie to turn around and come get us. By the end of the week, though, our packs were lighter, we'd met some interesting people, and we had some great stories.

I was very ready to get back home, but the longer we hiked, the more energized and content Whistler gradually became. On our last morning, he actually said, "I feel like I could hike forever."

The next few years, Brian joined us on our week-long, summer-time section hikes. We pushed the limits of how many pink-lemonade refills they would serve in hiker-friendly restaurants (I'm not certain there *is* a limit, but I think our record was four gallons).

When I went off to college, our section hikes stopped, but as it turned out, Whistler's AT bug had never been fully cured, but had lain dormant for years—until he started reading about other thru-hikers. And researching new packs. And freeze-dried soups. And driving long distances to meet up with, and pick the brains of, former thru- hikers. And physically conditioning himself by going on ten-plus-mile trail/ shore hikes and up thousands of flights of stairs. And then suddenly Annie and my brother and our families were driving to drop him off at Springer Mountain to begin his journey. And you are about to share in the adventure.

My dad started his trail journal online with the intention of jour-naling every day, and he did it. And it was good! Many of us checked and read it every morning, thanks to fancy modern technology. And we worried a little on mornings when no post had been uploaded, thanks to the *limitations* of fancy modern technology. It was fun to read—an odyssey of friendship, injury, odd-shelter mates, miniature ponies, and full-sized bears. The journal was so interesting and compelling that people who had never met the man started reading and following his journey (198,125 views as of February 25, 2018—trust me, he doesn't know that many people). Someone I'd never met approached me at my daughter's end-of-school program in South Carolina and asked if I was Whistler's son. I'm not kidding.

They say that "everyone hikes their own hike." It's a way of re-minding us not to judge hikers who do it differently or at a different pace than we do. But I can't imagine a more perfect hike for my dad than the one he had. Reading through his adventures, it's hard to find an AT experience he missed. Anyone looking for a list of what not to miss while hiking the Appalachian Trail may not need a source other than this book. The man who felt like he could hike forever did it—and he did it with style.

Richard Monk
February 25, 2018

Introduction

I'm not extraordinary, but I did an extraordinary thing. I thru-hiked the Appalachian Trail. Truth be told, I consider myself to be pretty average. Average weight, height, build, and of average intelligence (if I do say so myself). I've worked hard my whole life, and I raised two great, young men with my wife of thirty-eight years, Ann Marie. At fifty-seven, I found myself ready to take on one of my lifelong goals. I would often mention to Ann Marie that *if* I ever hiked the Appalachian Trail (AT), this, that, and the other thing, but, Annie (my pet name for Ann Marie) would always correct me and say, "*When* you hike the Appalachian Trail."

My definitive commitment to meet my self-imposed goal was made in the fall of 2016. It happened quite innocently, and was perhaps somewhat unplanned, as I found myself relentlessly reading everything I could lay my hands on about the nearly 2,200-mile trek. Sure, I've hiked a lot in my life, and had previously hiked about three hundred miles of the AT, back when my sons were teenagers. We lived in Georgia and South Carolina at the time, and my sons and I would do a section of the trail each summer together. I had, back then, imprinted on my brain that I had a thru-hike in me, so here I was, at a good place in my life and with the full support of my wife, ready to hike the AT.

It was late in November of 2016 that I made a decision to journal my hike with the help of trailjournals.com. I knew I would want to document my journey, including my preparation, for several reasons. I knew I'd want a way for my friends and family to follow along on this journey, but more importantly, I knew I would hold myself accountable if I committed to writing my journal entries each day.

Another benefit to writing them each day was that doing so served as the basis for this book. Preparation and planning involved reading numerous books on the AT, including a good number of them written by authors who had themselves previously hiked the AT. I would find myself struggling to sleep with this constant hunger for information on the AT. I was devouring book after book and gleaning all that I could, while knowing that everything I learned from those who had blazed the trail before me would move me closer to achieving a successful thru-hike.

In addition to gaining knowledge, I also understood the importance of being physically prepared for this monumental feat. I set myself up on an exercise regimen that would aid in my success. My physical preparation focused on the obvious leg strengthening, but also building upper body strength. I live in Nova Scotia, where the winters can be pretty harsh. I spent many hours with my full pack on my back going up and down our stairs. This allowed me to continue my exercise regimen indoors while there was deep snow outside. I dubbed this exercise "uppa-downs," a term I borrowed from my granddaughter, Katy Ellis, who would always reach up and say "uppa-down" when she wanted to be picked up. Speaking of snow, there is really no better workout than shoveling that white stuff.

I would also read other hikers' trail journals. It wouldn't be unusual to find me at my laptop reading trailjournals.com, coffee in hand at three in the morning. This was when I found myself second-guessing some of my decisions that I thought I had long since worked out. With so much information out there, you can start to go a bit crazy. How the first thru-hikers ever succeeded is a mystery to me. You obviously want to have all the "plus" boxes checked, and want to avoid checking the "negative" boxes. The problem is that if you research long enough, you find conflicting information and suggestions.

Mail drops happened to be the most confusing issue for me. Allow me to first explain what a "mail drop" is. There are literally hundreds of places you can have supplies mailed to along the AT. Post offices, outfitters, motels and hiker hostels will accept and hold packages mailed to them when identified for a thru-hiker on the mailing address. Several extensive lists are available online along with particulars such as whether the receiver charges a fee for holding your package to how many days they will hold it. Different schools of thought exist out there, everything from "don't sweat it, as it will work itself out" to advance food drops along the entire AT—and everything in-between. I eventually found myself leaning toward re-supplying as I went, with supplementing eight to ten mail drops for those areas that are logistically difficult to re-supply.

What's in a name? Picture yourself walking away from life as you know it today. You leave everything behind that makes you who you are and how you are identified when you take those first steps on the AT. Well, long distance hikers leave their given names behind too. You will now have a new identity, the identity of a hiker, a hiker with a new name...a trail name. Trail names are a funny thing, and are not to be taken lightly. Two schools of thought exist when it comes to taking a trail name: first, it can be bestowed upon you by your fellow hikers; or the other option is to choose a name for yourself. A character trait, flaw, or particular peculiar tendency can be used by your fellow hikers to give you your trail name, which can be dangerous. Just imagine having to hike 2,200 miles with a name that you really hate. Giving yourself a trail name, however, is frowned upon by some in the hiking community. Nonetheless, that is what I did. My trail name is Whistler—I whistle a lot, plain and simple.

Springer Mountain—how I got there. The majority of thru-hikers start at the southern terminus of the trail at Springer Mountain. Some will do the approach trail that starts at Amicalola Falls State Park, while others start at Springer Mountain. I've done the 7.5-mile approach trail on two previous section hikes, but elected to skip it for my thru-hike (it's not part of the AT). I asked my son Richard if he might give me a lift and drop me off at Springer Mountain when it came time for me to start my hike. I try to not be a burden on my family, especially since both of our sons have young families and are obviously all very busy with their lives. Well, I found out just how blessed I am.

Lauren, Richard's wife, took charge and booked a cabin close to Amicalola State Park for Ann Marie, myself, Richard, Lauren, and my granddaughters. My other son Brian, and his wife, Sarah, live another couple hours further away, and again, I didn't want to burden them. They have their two boys, ages two and three months, and Sarah had just returned to work after three months of maternity leave. Well, the good Lord blessed me again. They also came to see me off. Life just couldn't get any better. My hike had just become a true family affair. With a free afternoon before I actually started my hike I thought it would be a good idea to take my granddaughters for a trip to Woody Gap so they could learn what it means to be a trail angel and to hand out trail magic to those hikers that were already on the trail. Trail angels can be anyone who has hiked, know someone who hikes or just love the idea of supporting hikers by providing trail magic. Trail magic can be food, snacks, drink or any random act of kindness, all of which I personally experienced while on my thru-hike and that of which you will read about in the following pages.

What follows on these pages is my experience and the story of my thru-hike. For those that may not know, a thru-hike is the completion of a long trail such as the 2,189 miles of the AT in a single season. You will get a serious and up-close glimpse into the life of a thru-hiker. No two hikes could ever be the same, but I believe my hike is a true example of what one could expect to encounter during those approximate five million steps required to complete one of the world's greatest long trails.

DAY 1

THE REST OF THIS HIKE HAS TO BE EASIER THAN IT WAS TODAY

11.5 Miles Hiked; 11.5 Miles Total
Start: Springer Mountain; End: Stealth Camp, Sassafras Mountain

Parting Is Such Sweet Sorrow.

The drive to Springer Mountain was an adventure all on its own. Driving the back country roads to the coveted starting point of my adventure was exciting for me, while a bit nerve-racking for the rest of the family. My sons and their families drove in their vehicles, while Annie and I drove in our rental car. The dirt and gravel roads were winding and pocked with potholes big enough to swallow a vehicle whole. There was so much rattling that I was certain that a few essential nuts and bolts must have been leaving a trail we could follow back, thus ensuring we wouldn't get lost.

We arrived at the Springer Mountain parking lot at around ten thirty that morning and took the 0.9-mile hike southbound to the

3,782-foot summit of Springer Mountain so we could take pictures and I could sign the thru-hikers registration book. It was a beautiful day for a hike, and little three-year-old Katy Ellis led the way. Her energy had me convinced that perhaps the wrong person was about to take on this 2,200-mile trek. After this precious family time together, we all hiked back to our cars, and after a prayer for safe travel, everyone but Annie took off for their respective homes.

The weekend leading up to my departure far exceeded my expectations, and served as a reminder of how blessed I am. Annie had let me know that she wanted to hike north with me for a bit, and after about a half mile, we sat along the trail's edge and enjoyed our lunch together. This would be our last meal together for a long time—a very long time. After lunch, it was time . . . time for me to walk away. Having to say goodbye to my beautiful bride of thirty-eight years made, for what I knew, would be the most difficult day of my journey. But I did it, I walked away, and it was difficult—incredibly difficult, indeed.

There were obviously a number of other folks on the trail, but I don't believe I met anyone more determined than I was. You see, I was on a mission, a mission to finish what I started. I always finish what I start, and knowing that about myself convinced those who know me well enough that I would complete the 2,189 miles of the Appalachian Trail. There was no doubt in my mind that I would march through all fourteen states, and that I would be able to call myself a thru-hiker. Mount Katahdin was a very long way from where I found myself on that first day, but I knew each step would bring me closer to my goal. I did make some great time that day, as I hiked until it started to get dark around six that evening. I found the perfect stealth campsite at the top of Sassafras Mountain (3,300 feet). I hiked a total of 11.5 miles that first day, which wasn't too bad, considering my late start. As reference, the term "stealth camp" defines a campsite that is not designated as a campsite. They are not at a designated shelter area or approved sites and are sometimes forbidden especially in some states and some of the national parks I hiked through.

I fixed a simple dinner and washed it down with a beer that had found its way into my pack. (Thanks for that, Richard; it was well worth the twelve ounces of added weight.) I crawled into my tent and thought about my first day on the Appalachian Trail. I thought about how blessed I was to have a supportive family. I thought of how blessed I was to have Annie in my life, and how difficult it was to walk away from the girl I'd married thirty-eight years earlier. It was at that moment that I decided I hadn't walked away from Annie—I had taken my first steps back to her.

DAY 2
My New Best Friends

17 Miles Hiked; 28.5 Miles Total
Start: Sassafras Mountain; End: Slaughter Creek Trail

Whistler and His Two Best Friends.

My decision and determination to keep a daily journal was going to take a serious commitment. It was only my second day of hiking and

I was so tired and not at all in the mood to document my day, but I knew I'd regret it if I didn't. Using trailjournals.com to journal via my smart phone wasn't how I usually rolled, and it was a bit of a stretch for me. As a general rule, I'm not big into social media. Personally, I have a difficult time with putting myself out there for the world to see, but my family and friends had shown great interest in my endeavour, and I figured that posting my daily progress and experiences might even be of interest to myself someday when I chose to look back.

So here was day number two: After an early dinner the night before, and in my sleeping bag by eight-thirty, I was up by four in the morning, packed, and already hiking by six in a light rain. While hiking, I met "Captain Handy," a recently retired Florida highway patrol officer, just before Justus Creek, and we hiked together until Gooch Mountain Shelter, where I had my second breakfast and coffee. I know it was a bit early in my thru-hike for "hiker hunger" to set in, but that second breakfast and cup of java was screaming my name. Captain Handy hiked on, but we leapfrogged pretty much all day, so I, like most thru-hiker wannabes, was a bit unsure about committing to hiking with a comrade.

There is so much to consider when deciding if you really want to hike with someone you already know, let alone hiking with a perfect stranger. The obvious questions arise: Will we get along all right? Will they slow me down, or perhaps make me feel obligated to go faster than I really want to go? If things don't feel right, can I leave without any hard feelings? If I hike with a friend, will they still be my friend after the hike is over? It's so difficult to say, but at that point, I liked *me*, and I like hiking by myself. I enjoy the solitude, the quiet peaceful time to myself, and the mindless, one-foot-in-front-of-the-other task at hand is familiar and also comforting to me.

I made it to Woody Gap by a quarter past eleven that morning, and had an early lunch at the same picnic tables where my granddaughters and I had sat just two days earlier while we handed out trail magic. This is a popular pull-off for the beautiful overlook/view, and for day hikers looking for an enjoyable and accessible hike. I enjoyed watching the people from a distance, and more importantly, I enjoyed the time to myself. After lunch, I hiked on, and made it to Slaughter Creek that afternoon by a quarter past four and called it a day. That was a respectable seventeen miles I'd hiked, and with tender feet, I found a great creek, perfect for soaking my dogs . . . they be some tired.

Back to my early morning start: I couldn't sleep, so why not hike instead? It was pitch dark when I started that morning, so I had to use my headlamp. It was so quiet, peaceful, and—yes—lonely. But that was okay; lonely isn't always a bad thing. I did take one wrong turn, but quickly got myself re-oriented and back on the trail. That was all I needed—to have gotten lost on my second day. What a headline that would have been.

Now, about my new best friends: Those who know me, and who have perhaps hiked with me, know I have always used a hiking staff. After much research, I'd thought I would use trekking poles on this trip, and boy, was that the right decision. They had already saved me from several falls. Just as important, is the reduction of stress on the legs, especially the knees. Walking with trekking poles requires deliberate and purposeful movements. On flat surfaces (not too many of those on the AT) you actually push off through your steps. On the uphill climbs, you are pushing down using your upper body. The use of trekking poles on descents helps with your stability and helps carry some of the load—almost like having four legs. Trekking poles were my new best friends.

Day 3

You Ain't My Friends No More

9.9 Miles Hiked; 38.4 Miles Total
Start: Slaughter Creek Trail; End: Whitley Gap Shelter

The Boot Tree at Neel Gap.

The day started a bit later than what I had hoped. I woke at two thirty, and thought I would never get back to sleep, but the next thing I knew, it was five thirty in the morning. I broke camp, had breakfast, and was hiking by seven. The weather was awful that day, with rain and fog the whole time. I really can't remember the last time I was so wet. Blood Mountain was in my sights first thing that morning, and would prove to be a formidable adversary. The name "Blood Mountain" sounds intimidating: Blood Mountain . . . Blood Mountain . . . it hurts just saying it. At 4,458 feet, and the highest mountain within the Georgia portion of the AT (sixth highest in the state of Georgia overall), it really isn't as bad as it sounds. Plus, I had hiked this mountain twice before with my sons, and knew what to expect.

That morning, I was on the summit in a heavy fog by eight o'clock, and unfortunately, I'd snapped one of my trekking poles on the way up. I shared already the fact that my trekking poles had become my new best friends, and that morning I had some pretty strong words for them. Fortunately for me, Neel Gap and Mountain Crossings, an outfitters, were just a few miles ahead. Upon my arrival, the people at the outfitters were very sympathetic, and especially happy to sell me some new best friends. This was where I picked up my first mail drop, which I'd mailed to myself a week prior to the start of my hike. After a short time at Neel Gap, I was already itching to move on. The weather was awful, with a light, cold rain and a heavy fog that lingered. Unlike the other hikers who were taking shelter, I needed to keep moving. My mantra had already been determined, spoken silently to myself, and it was one I was prepared to follow: *No rain, no Maine.*

To that end, believe it or not, sometimes you actually have to think while hiking. There are decisions that *do* need to be made, like, do I have peanut butter or tuna on that tortilla for lunch? Should I get water at this creek or at the next one? Well, that day I had to decide if I should continue to hike in the rain or call it quits. Why was this such a difficult decision to make? Well, Whitley Gap Shelter happens to be 1.2 miles off the trail—that's why. That meant I would hike 1.2 miles to the shelter and would have to hike 1.2 miles back to the trail the next day. I, like most thru-hikers, would ordinarily never consider hiking that far off the trail, and to be honest, it was a mistake on my part—and one I can promise I will not make again.

It was five thirty by then, and I'd already had dinner and was tucked deep in my sleeping bag. It was cold and wet out there, with a big storm on the way that evening, but I was safe, warm, and dry. I thought, *Let's see how this REI quarter-dome tent holds up tonight.*

About Neel Gap and Mountain Crossings outfitters: Located directly on the trail at Neel Gap, this outfitters is a thru-hiker's dream come true. There is really nothing that you can't find here. Name-brand hiking/outdoor equipment, snacks, full re-supply, fuel, phone charging station, and anything else your heart desires. Mail drops are accepted, with a recommended dollar donation for the service. There's a full service hostel, cabins for rent, a shuttle service, and full shake-down service as well. I watched as one of their shakedown experts sat on the floor with a thru-hiker and went through the hiker's entire pack to assist them in reducing its weight.

While it was true that I (like most thru-hikers) had only been on the trail for three days, I had no problem indulging in a sugary drink and high-calorie snack. It's estimated that 10 percent of the hikers that make it to Neel Gap will quit and come off trail there. Reasons vary, anywhere from injury to the hike not being what they'd thought it was going to be—and all reasons in-between. In any case, Neel Gap is a logical exit point for those who decide thru-hiking is not for them.

Day 4

Right Place, Right Time?

14.4 Miles Hiked; 52.9 Miles Total
Start: Whitley Gap Shelter; End: Unicoi Gap

Sometimes It Really Is a Walk in the Woods.

When I woke up that morning at four thirty, I found myself to be insanely hungry, so I decided it was time to get my day going. I thought I'd solve the hunger issue first, so I grabbed my headlamp and crawled out of my fine accommodations for my food bag, which was hanging on one of the nearby bear cables at Whitley Gap Shelter. I pulled out a Pop-Tart (frosted strawberry . . . a superb pastry) and thought to myself that it was way too cold and way too windy to hike in the dark, so I put my head down on my inflatable Sea to Summit pillow (this forty five dollar blow-up pillow was positively one of my best investments) and slept until six thirty.

I jumped up, packed, and was hiking by seven that monring. The weather was bone-chillingly cold, but beautiful and sunny. I made it to Low

Gap Shelter by a quarter past ten, and had the place to myself. My second breakfast/early lunch consisted of tortillas and peanut butter with Starbucks instant coffee (heaven on earth). My plan was to finish up at Blue Mountain Shelter, but I got there way too early and decided to hike on (gotta make hay while the sun shines). I decided I'd head to Blue Mountain Camp, which was just another 0.9 miles. Not sure how, but I missed it by 0.6 miles. Hikers never go backwards if they can avoid doing so, so I hiked on to Unicoi Gap (another 1.5 miles). When I got to Unicoi, Georgia Highway 75, a young man with the trail name "Bunn" was there waiting on a shuttle.

It wasn't long before I got to the Hiawassee Budget Inn to share a forty-five-dollar room, get a hot shower, and have a Subway sandwich for dinner (we didn't share the sub or the shower . . . just the cost of the room). Right place, right time.

A random thought: the AT crosses a highway every few days or so. You can hear cars and trucks long before you exit the woods and cross that road. I've noticed how excited I get while still deep in the woods when I can hear those passing vehicles. I'm not really sure why I get so excited, but I think it's all about still feeling somewhat connected to the real world. As I hike on and beyond those crossing roads, the traffic noise fades and I get excited. I'm not sure why, but I think it's because I'll soon find myself disconnected from the real world.

About the town of Hiawassee: Hiawassee is a small town of two square miles with a population of just under a thousand. The name "Hiawassee" is said to be of either Cherokee or Creek origin, and means "meadow." This hikers' retreat sits close to the northern-most border of Georgia, just before entering North Carolina. Easy accessibility by shuttle or hitch and resupply opportunities, including fast food restaurants, make this small town a desirable respite.

So what ever happened to the hiker named Bunn?

This young, twenty-something hiker stayed behind the next morning, and to be honest, I doubt Bunn ever returned to the trail. It's impossible to look at a person and know whether or not they have what it takes to commit to a thru-hike. Hikers come in all sorts of shapes and sizes, which means that a visual first impression should be the last method used to determine a person's likelihood of success. Let's just say that some are more interested in what they can put in their pipe than meeting the challenges of a thru-hike on the AT.

DAY 5

A LESSON LEARNED WHILE ATTENDING THE SCHOOL OF HIKE-OLOGY

12.3 Miles Hiked; 65.2 Miles Total
Start: Unicoi Gap; End: Kelly Knob

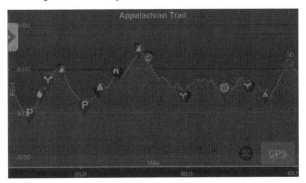

GPS/Guthook Screenshot, Elevation of Today's Hike.

The Budget Inn was exactly what you would expect for forty-five dollars, but, it had a real bed with clean sheets (I convinced myself that the sheets were clean; Bunn slept in his sleeping bag). I woke up at five and did some housekeeping. I dragged my pack into the bathroom so as to not disturb my roommate. First on the to-do list was to fix my rain pants. They kept falling off me, so I had to rig the elastic to stay cinched. Next on the list: When I first woke up I felt some pain in my small toe. Upon closer inspection, I discovered that someone seemed to have taken my toe and replaced it with another one, an unfamiliar toe (invasion of the toe snatchers?). This toe was obviously not mine, as it was completely out of proportion to the rest of my foot. After all, I'd had that toe for fifty-seven years and could tell the difference. I decided the best course of action was to stick it with my knife. Once I did this, it seemed to deflate and then eventually turned into my toe again. I wrapped that piggy in medical tape and was ready to roll.

After I was finished getting my things together, the shuttle took me back to Unicoi Gap a half hour later, at nine thirty—which gave me another late start, but such is life on the trail. As I hiked along, I met a fellow hiker named Tin Man (no scarecrow or cowardly lion yet, though). I obviously had to ask why that was his trail name. He replied that he was on a celebratory hike. You see, Tin Man had/has a heart condition, and was actually seeing a heart transplant specialist when he'd made a recovery that doctors still can't explain. I'll come back to Tin Man in a bit.

Then that imposter of a little toe started acting up again. The little fellow next to him started some nonsense, too, so I took my boot and sock off and stabbed him with my knife—really, I did. With both those suckers now wrapped in medical tape, I put my sock and boot back on and started hiking . . . hiking real slow. Re-enter Tin Man—yep, the guy with the bad heart, pacemaker, and a defibrillator surgically implanted in his chest. He was cranking along, while I was all worked up over a couple of stupid blisters. Well, I decided to let Mr. Pacemaker set the pace. We cranked out some fast miles. I finally told Tin Man that I couldn't keep up, and that he should go on ahead. That's when he let me know what he did for a living: He was a personal trainer. Anyway, I caught up with him a bit later, and we camped on top of Kelly Knob that night.

Thank you, Tin Man, for helping lend some perspective to my hike.

DAY 6

THAT'S ONE STATE DOWN, THIRTEEN TO GO

13.4 Miles Hiked; 78.6 Miles Total
Start: Kelly Knob; End: Bly Gap

One State Down, Thirteen to Go.

While on top of Kelly Knob the previous night, Tin Man and I had experienced a huge thunder and lightning storm. There we were, in the most glorious of places, on a four-thousand-foot mountain, when all heck broke loose around ten o'clock. Not the smartest place to be, but it was quite the pyrotechnics show.

We packed our wet and muddy tents along with the rest of our gear when things calmed down around eight in the morning, which made for another unavoidable late start. We eventually stopped at Deep Gap Shelter and had breakfast. Our primary goal was to get to Dick's Creek Gap for trail magic. We knew of this supposed "trail magic" by way of the "trail" communications network. Lets just say that news travels quickly on the trail—especially when it has to do with food. When we arrived at Dick's Creek, we found a smorgasbord of hot dogs, bacon and eggs, soda, cookies, apples, snickers, MoonPies, and orange juice. Thank you, trail angels, Bigfoot and Greeter—that was awesome!

While partaking in this seemingly unlimited bounty, I learned that Bigfoot had thru-hiked the year prior. He (like most thru-hikers) has a true passion for the hiking community, and he would tell you that this was his way of giving back. FYI, Bigfoot also has a great series of YouTube videos that are instructive and helpful if you are planning a thru-hike. You can also follow him at followbigfoot.com. Lastly, Greeter was going to be starting his flip-flop thru-hike in two weeks.

We cranked out 13.4 miles that day, and set up at Bly Gap, North Carolina! So that was one state down, and thirteen to go. My feet had held up great, my stomach was full, my camp was set, and my sleeping bag was waiting for me.

A side note: I give my sincere thanks to all those who signed my guest book while I was on my hike. It meant so much to hear from family, friends, and strangers as they followed my personal journey. Special thanks to all the trail angels who provide random acts of kindness. The biggest call-out goes to those volunteers who give selflessly of their time and talents to maintain the trail so that we can enjoy their gifts.

WHEN DOES A WALK BECOME A HIKE?

When does a walk become a hike?
What satisfies, defines our likes?
The tromping, the climbing?
The tripping, the declining?
The pains, the distance?
The rains and resistance?
Or is it the release we feel
As our souls do heal?
Our steps are not simply random,
But placed in faith and in perfect tandem.
Our purpose and might, be it given,
Is certain and strong and keeps us driven.

(March, 10, 2017, Day 6)

Day 7

A CONTRAST OF BLACK AND WHITE

15.3 Miles Hiked; 93.9 Miles Total
Start: Bly Gap; End: Carter Gap Shelter

A Contrast of Black and White.

Tin Man and I left Bly Gap by a quarter to eight that morning—and a very cold morning it was. In fact, I don't believe it ever got above freezing that day. The climb out was insane, at what seemed like a nearly vertical ascent. We ended up separated with a plan to meet for lunch at Standing Indian Shelter, but as I learned later, Tin Man had missed the side trail to Standing Indian, and he kept going. We ended up meeting at Carter Gap Shelter that evening.

Because I had hiked most of the day by myself, I'd had time to think and take in what was going on around me. Let's just say, it wasn't pretty. The section of the AT I'd hiked that day was part of the area that had been devastated by horrific fires the year before. There is really no way to describe the destruction I witnessed. It was, quite honestly, difficult to walk through, and somewhat depressing. To have gone from seeing absolute beauty one day, to seeing pure devastation the next day, was a huge contrast.

This contradiction was made even more evident when it started to snow. This snow almost looked like ashes from the fire that were floating back to the scene of the inferno. This deeply blackened and charred forest juxtaposed with the heavy, white snow was a true contrast of black and white.

DAY 8

ONE WEEK ON THE TRAIL AND MORE THAN A HUNDRED MILES IN THE BOOKS

16.2 Miles Hiked; 110.1 Miles Total
Start: Carter Gap Shelter; End: Stealth Camp

Baby, It's Cold Outside.

That morning started out with freezing temperatures and three inches of snow. It was extremely difficult to motivate myself to creep out of my sleeping bag. To top it off, I'd lost time because the clocks had moved forward one hour for daylight saving time. Well, I finally got it moving; two maple-cinnamon oatmeal packets with dehydrated apples and a cup of coffee for breakfast sure helped. When I finally broke camp, which required me to remove as much snow and ice off everything that I could, it was 8:50 a.m.

I guess the good Lord had decided to rectify the issue of the scorched forest by covering it with a full blanket of snow. It was beautiful.

As the day went on and temperatures climbed, snow clods started falling on my head and down between my back and backpack. It started to get old after the countless times it had occurred. I knew come June I would have loved to have had that snow drop on me—why is it that we are never satisfied?

I hiked mostly solo that day, which gave me time to think before I later hit the one-hundred-mile mark. I thought about how, if God had been waiting at that one-hundred-mile mark to tell me I was done, no more hiking for Whistler, I didn't think I could have borne not being able to continue. Every mile I get to hike is precious to me, and I thank God for that privilege.

Okay, a suggestion for future thru-hikers with regard to my hike that day: When you get to Albert Mountain, fold up those trekking poles, stash them in your pack, and be ready for a rock scramble. It was especially tough-going with the snow and ice that day. I recommend three points of contact on that very steep and icy climb.

Another hiking tip: When it comes to a choice of sleeping bags, if you think you can get by with a three-season sleeping bag, forget it. The number one complaint I heard on my hike was how cold it was and how hard it was to get good sleep. I'd slept the past three nights in snow, freezing rain, and thunder storms, and I was always comfortable and warm. If you're concerned about your pack weight, give up something else to lighten the load. Pack the right sleeping bag for the conditions in which you'll be hiking.

Whatever happened to Tin Man?

He and I separated and hiked on, each at our own pace. I liked putting in longer days, which included a higher number of miles as well. We did stay in touch by way of text over the course of our respective hikes, but we eventually lost contact, unfortunately. With that said, I am very thankful that I met this fine gentleman, and I hold him in the highest regard and truly believe he came to me when I needed his inspiration.

Day 9

WATCH EVERY STEP YOU TAKE

17.4 Miles Hiked; 127.4 Miles Total
Start: Stealth Camp; End: Rocky Bald

Watch Every Step You Take.

Another freezing cold night—but I was warm in my four-seasons duck-down sleeping bag. There was a pattern happening that had come to my attention: My biggest problem had been breaking down camp each morning. There had been so much snow and ice to contend with that it was difficult to get it all off my tent each morning. I ended up packing it and carrying the extra weight. In fact, after hiking all day, I was having to shake it off my tent while making camp each evening.

There was so much ice on the trail that morning that it made for dangerous hiking conditions. With every step, I thought to myself that a slip or fall could be a hike-ending slip or fall. In addition to that, the trail tended to only be around eighteen to twenty-four inches wide in areas. There were places where I had to hug the mountainside because eighteen inches away was a drop to nothingness. Still, I was able to clock in another 17.4 miles that day—not too bad, considering the rough terrain and poor weather conditions.

The next day I would be heading to the Nantahala Outdoor Center to pick up a mail drop that my trail angel sister had mailed there for me. I was going to make it a "nero day," a day where only a few miles are hiked (a "zero day" is when you take a day off completely). I was looking forward to a real bed, and I would maybe even throw in a shower (or two) and laundry, as well.

The rest of that day's story,

I didn't originally write in my journal, as I didn't want to worry my wife and family. That afternoon, "Fish" and "Radio" (two terrific, twenty-something-year-old men who I'd been leapfrogging for several days) had come up behind me, and were hiking at their normal, quick pace. They'd told me about some bad weather that was coming our way. Apparently, freezing rain, snow, and high winds were expected. I'd already spent the last two nights in similar weather while everyone else had run off to Franklin. My thought had been that the tough weather would prepare me for the "Whites" of New Hampshire later on.

Well, to be honest, I was tired of waking up each morning and packing a frozen tent. I decided I would make a run for Cold Spring

Shelter, six miles further up the trail, and gain one of the six shelter spots for myself. I gotta tell you, I was practically running. Imagine my disappointment when I arrived and found eight people (including Fish and Radio) in a shelter designed for six. It was still early (four o'clock in the afternoon) and I still had some steam in my legs, so I decided to do a couple more miles instead. My goal was to get to Rocky Bald.

When I took the side trail to Rocky Bald, I did so with a clear trail that had no snow yet. I climbed the stone-faced bald and followed the blue blazes (the AT is marked with white blazes that measure two inches by six inches while side trails are marked with blue blazes of the same dimensions) to what I thought was a perfect tentsite, and one with spectacular views. I knew there was snow in the forecast, but I really should have taken it more seriously than I did. The snowfall was heavy and kept me up throughout the night because I had to keep pushing up on my tent from inside to keep the snow accumulation to a minimum.

When I woke up that morning and looked outside, I was shocked by what I saw. The snow was deep, which would make getting off the bald and finding my way back to the trail extremely difficult. I'm not going to sugarcoat it—I was fearful for my safety. I had made a huge error in judgement by climbing that bald, granite, five-thousand-foot summit, and had placed myself in a really bad situation. The blue blazes had been painted on the stone that was now covered with a foot of snow. The tree limbs were heavy with snow and hid anything that looked remotely like a trail. To top it off, the overnight freezing temperatures had discharged my cell phone. I knew this was bad, really bad. Of course, my first thought was what the headline would look like, perhaps something like this: "Spring Thaw Reveals Lost Hiker."

I sat in my tent and made a step-by-step plan for how I would get myself out of the mess in which I had now found myself.

Eating and drinking something hot was first on my survival plan; dress warmly was next, and finally—break camp. I made my way by instinct, not by following a blazed trail. I tried to use recall from the climb the night before, but it had been getting dark when I'd arrived, and nothing looked familiar now. At times I was on all fours as I crawled under those heavy, wet, snow-laden tree branches, cautiously trying to make my way down the ice- and snow-covered bald in search of the trail.

Well, I made it back to the trail, but I'd learned yet another valuable lesson in the process: Mother nature is tough, and she can be unforgiving, but at the end of the day, I'm responsible for my own safety—and I had better be thinking of all the what-ifs.

Day 10

OH, TO SLEEP IN A REAL BED

9.9 Miles Hiked; 137.3 Miles Total
Start: Rocky Bald; End: Nantahala Outdoor Center

View from Rocky Bald.

So there I was, enjoying a glass of red wine—thanks to my dear, eccentric sister/trail angel, Susan and her drop box full of surprises—as I thought about the day's events. I'd made the 9.9 miles to the Nantahala Outdoor Center in exactly four hours, mostly descending. In fact, over that 9.9 miles, the trail went from 5,030 feet to 1,732 feet. Ice and snow had made it a real challenge, and had me slipping and falling three times. I kept my speed up, as I had factored in the soft snow, and the toque on my head was assurance of a limited impact any concussion would have if my head hit a rock on one of my falls.

I arrived safely to the Center, and made my way to what is referred to as the "stone house" to see about that night's accommodations. The room was a bit expensive, but I probably would have paid any price to be able to sleep in a warm and dry room with a real bed.

The building they placed me in was set up with semi-private rooms that had bunk beds and common areas, including a living room, kitchen, shared bathrooms, and laundry room. I believe there are eight rooms in this building, but I was the only person there, so it was peacefully quiet. My room had a huge, wooden beam that ran below the ceiling, and was perfect for hanging up my wet tent to dry. After getting myself situated, I walked over to the riverside restaurant and ordered a big, fat hamburger, fries, and two of the best beers I've ever had the pleasure of drinking.

The Appalachian Trail passes directly through the Nantahala Outdoor Center's property, making it an obvious place to take a break, grab a bite, and perhaps take a room for the evening. The Center offers whitewater rafting trips, courses on kayak and canoe paddling, along with bike rentals, ropes courses, fly fishing, and kayak touring. The Nantahala river is used by Olympic paddlers for their training with courses laid out on this fast water. They also have a full outfitters shop and a fantastic restaurant. The Nantahala Outdoor Center holds a special place in my heart, with fond memories of the time my sons and I stopped and stayed there many years earlier when we'd section hiked the AT.

DAY 11

WHISTLING A HAPPY TUNE

6.7 Miles Hiked; 144 Miles Total
Start: Nantahala Outdoor Center; End: Sassafras Gap Shelter

Score! Free Hiker Breakfast.

Spending the night at the Nantahala Outdoor Center was a great move (more luck on my part, than anything). I woke up at six, revived and raring to go. I had stayed in my room all afternoon and evening the day before so I could get my gear, clothes, and myself cleaned up. My plan was to get a big breakfast at the Outdoor Center's restaurant, River's End. I walked over to the restaurant, went inside, and grabbed a seat. I saw a huge group of about twenty-plus people off to one side, which turned out to be a group preparing for a river paddle (and you thought I was crazy).

Anyway, they were having breakfast off a big buffet, so I asked a gentleman, who was apparently the manager, if I might be able to order breakfast. He apologized, and informed me of their seasonal hours; unfortunately, they were only open from eleven to seven, so I was too early. But in the next breath, he told me to go grab a plate and help myself from the group's buffet! Life is freaking *awesome* sometimes. Good karma for Mr. Restaurant Manager at the Nantahala Outdoor Center.

The hike out of Bryce was going straight up. It snowed so much the night before, that it was up over my knees in places. When I arrived at Sassafras Gap Shelter, which was just 6.4 miles of hiking, I had lunch and decided that it would have been irresponsible and dangerous to continue. A very short day, but at twenty-four degrees, I felt I had made a good decision.

I had a full food bag, all my layers on, and a group of fellow hikers including a ridgerunner (The Appalachian Trail Conservancy employs ridgerunners to help educate hikers on proper hiking etiquette and trail use.) to chew the fat with. It was supposed to warm up some the next day, so I would make up the miles then. In the meantime, I was safe and warm in my sleeping bag.

Day 12

OH, WHAT A NIGHT

15.2 Miles Hiked; 159.2 Miles Total
Start: Sassafras Gap Shelter; End: Cable Gap Shelter

Clear Skies after the Storm.

It was a very long and cold night for us inhabitants of Sassafras Gap Shelter. As I explained before, freezing temperatures forced us to stay put. In fact, it got down to nine degrees outside. When I thought about it, I realized that I would have been warmer sleeping in my freezer at home—so crazy cold! It was so cold that my isobutane stove wouldn't ignite until I warmed the canister with my body heat underneath my clothes. While I'd been hiking to Sassafras, my hydration system would freeze. I would have to warm the hose and bite valve with my hands and breath to thaw them whenever I needed a drink.

The shelter was big enough to sleep fourteen, but there were only six of us (nobody else was crazy enough to be out in that weather), and everyone was inside their sleeping bags by one in the afternoon. I had every piece of clothing I had with me on my body. At around midnight, I needed to visit the privy, and found that my boots were frozen solid. I slept with my hydration bladder along with my water filter in my sleeping bag to keep them from freezing.

That morning, all anyone wanted to do was to get hiking, as that was the only true way to stay warm. Fortunately, the day's temperatures were fantastic, and reached into the 40s, along with clear skies—praise the Lord. It was slow going, though, as there was snow and ice, which made hiking difficult and dangerous. I slipped and fell several times, even having used extreme caution.

Truth be told, it's possible that I may have passed some of the most spectacular views that day, but I would never have known it. I was too busy looking at my feet and deciding where to put them in order to keep myself from falling. Keeping myself upright seemed much more important than to even begin to think about the scenery around me. I'd be remiss if I didn't mention Jacob's Ladder. This climb was by far the most difficult I'd experienced since I'd started my epic journey on March 5. Jacob's Ladder wasn't exactly a biblical experience, but there were a lot of hikers, myself included, who were using the Lord's name in vain. There was no ladder there, no stairs, elevator or escalator, either; in fact, not even a couple of switchbacks to speak of. This was a vertical, unforgiving climb that will just beat you up. An alert for future hikers: shorten your trekking poles and get ready for this one.

Right at noon, Bottles, Carl, and myself met down at Stecoah Gap at North Carolina Highway 143, had lunch at a picnic table, and agreed to continue on to Cable Gap Shelter, which would make for a 15.2-mile day. I don't believe I ever ran into "Bottles" and "Carl" again while on my journey and never really got to know them. Was I too busy? Can you be too busy when all you are doing is hiking? I considered this a failing on my part and tried to commit myself and my time to my fellow hikers from that point forward. That put Fontana Dam at just over six miles away, where I was going to pick up my next mail drop with resupply, thanks to my daughter-in-law/trail angel, Lauren. From there, I would enter the Great Smoky Mountains National Park.

Day 13

I'm Okay

6.7 Miles Hiked; 165.9 Miles Total
Start: Cable Gap Shelter; End: Fontana Hilton Shelter

The Fontana Hilton Shelter.

I got an early start that morning at a quarter to eight, with a goal of getting to Fontana Village as soon as possible. I had my mail drop to pick up, had to print my permit for Smoky National Park, a real meal to eat, and some fuel and batteries to locate and purchase. My goal was to hike the twelve miles past Fontana Shelter (popular amongst thru-hikers and fondly named the "Fontana Hilton"), but the hours just slipped by. The park rule is that you are required stay at their shelters (no stealth camping allowed). I would have been too late getting in, so it was another nero day.

During that morning's hike, there was ice everywhere. I did everything I could not to slip, but still took three big spills. Each time I'd get back up and look around to make sure no one had seen me fall (like who would have been out there to see me?). I'd take full inventory to make sure I was still whole and would then say to myself—as my granddaughter Blakely says after a fall—"I'm okay." (Only, Blakely yells it out.)

When I arrived at the road crossing that led to Fontana Village, I called for a shuttle. I was picked up and then delivered to the lodge at Fontana Village, where I claimed my mail drop and made my way into the dining room for a hiker breakfast. After my appetite had been mostly satisfied, I returned to the front desk, where they assisted with printing my park permit.

Once I had purchased fuel and batteries at the general store, I grabbed the next shuttle back to the road crossing and hiked on to the Fontana Hilton. It was still early, but not early enough to make it to the next shelter.

Fontana Village Resort was originally built as a town for the workers and their families who came from all around the country to construct the Tennessee Valley Authority Fontana Dam. Construction of Fontana Dam began in 1942, and was completed in 1944. The dam was built to provide power for the war effort at the Oakridge, Tennessee Nuclear Facility, and to alleviate seasonal flooding in the greater Tennessee River Valley. Fontana Village is now a popular resort for family vacations, fishing, and water sports.

The Fontana Hilton is the name bestowed upon this above-average shelter by the hiking community. This shelter boasts two sides, two levels, a water pump, charging station, trash bins, fire pit, a washroom with a shower nearby, and a million-dollar view of Fontana Lake. It really is the perfect spot to overnight before crossing the dam and entering the Great Smoky Mountains National Park. Located at the bottom of the mountain below the Fontana Village Resort, the dam's visitor center records more than one hundred thousand guests each year who come to see the structure—the largest dam east of the Mississippi River. The dam is 480 feet high and stretches 2,365 feet across the Little Tennessee River.

DAY 14

THAT'S WHY THEY CALL THEM THE SMOKY MOUNTAINS

17.6 Miles Hiked; 183.5 Miles Total
Start: Fontana Hilton Shelter; End: Spence Field Shelter

That's Why They Call Them the Smoky Mountains.

Staying at the Fontana Hilton the night before ended up being a good decision. A heavy rain and fog dropped by to pay us a visit. It rained all night, which put me a little behind my self-imposed goal of a 7:00 a.m.

departure. I had really wanted to get in my first twenty-mile day, but had to settle for 17.6 miles. I was walking across the Fontana Dam at a quarter to eight, and was in awe of its enormity and what a wonder of engineering the structure was. I was quite amused by a sign that was posted, which read, "No Jumping or Diving." Really? Did they really have to post a sign?

Views were limited for most of the day, as that Great Smoky Mountain fog hung heavy. That was okay, though, because once again, I was too busy looking at my feet. What do you get when one day you have a foot of snow, and the next, a rain storm with temperatures in the 50s? You get mud that is the consistency of lard. Lots of slip-sliding—but fortunately, I had no falls.

As previously mentioned, while hiking in the Smoky Mountains National Park, you are required to stay at the shelters. The only way you can tent camp is if the shelter is full. In other words, you plan your entire day based on the distance you can hike from one shelter to the next shelter. No stealth camping can cramp your hiking style.

I was at Spence Field Shelter that night, which was packed (with a lot of people who were not very concerned about my desire to get rest). A couple more days, though, and I would be out of the Great Smoky Mountains National Park, with a bit more freedom. Don't get me wrong, the Smokies are beautiful, and the shelters are beautiful (stacked stone and timber construction). They are just a bit too constricting.

The Great Smoky Mountains National Park is made up of 522,419 acres, which makes it one of the largest protected areas in the eastern United States. The park itself was chartered by Congress in 1934, and was officially dedicated by President Franklin Delano Roosevelt in 1940. The park is the most visited park in America, with over eleven million recreational visitors each year, and is home to more than two hundred species of birds, fifty species of fish, thirty-nine species of reptiles, and forty-three species of amphibians. It is also notable that the black bear population at the park numbers somewhere around 1,500. There are over one hundred species of trees in the park, with lower elevations dominated by deciduous, leafy trees that at higher elevations give way to coniferous trees, like the Fraser fir. The park also boasts of being home to over 1,400 flowering plants and four thousand species of non-flowering plants, including those that are rare, and ones not found anywhere else.

While it's true that only seventy or so miles of the Appalachian Trail go through the park, there are over 850 miles of hiking trails that run through the Great Smoky Mountains.

DAY 15

FOUND NOT GUILTY FOR REASONS OF INSANITY

13.5 Miles Hiked; 197 Miles Total
Start: Spence Field Shelter; End: Double Spring Gap Shelter

The Hoarfrost We Hiked Through That Morning.

I would have been found innocent of my crime by the court of Spence Field Shelter, had I followed up on my desire to put an end to one of my shelter mate's snoring. Let's call him "Simpson" (he and his family resided in Simpsonville, South Carolina). He and I struck up a conversation because of his South Carolina Gamecock hat—a very nice guy for sure. Simpson was just preparing to finish his section hike, and shared his love for the AT with me.

When hiker midnight struck (around eight o'clock that night), everyone was getting settled. Simpson must have been real tired, as he quickly fell asleep. My imagination kicked into high gear when it became apparent that it was going to be a long and sleepless night. My first thought was that I could smother Simpson with his Sea to Summit blow-up pillow. I imagined the other twelve to fifteen shelter residents jumping up and applauding my actions. Court would have been held in the morning over our oatmeal, Pop-Tarts, and instant coffee. I believe I would have been found not guilty by reason of temporary insanity, and allowed to continue my hike. My next thought was that I would hike back to Fontana Dam and locate that sign I mentioned previously—"No Jumping or Diving"—and throw myself over the dam. That sign made a great deal of sense to me at that moment.

The next day's hike was treacherous, with ice along the trail in the morning after there had been freezing temperatures overnight. By midafternoon, the sun had worked its magic and turned the trail into a mixture of lard and quicksand. It was very slow going (no slips or falls for Whistler that day—whew). I was just a couple of miles from Clingmans Dome. At 6,643 feet, Clingmans Dome is the highest peak on the AT and in Smoky Mountains National Park, and the second highest mountain east of the Mississippi. I was hoping for a clear morning and some beautiful views.

One of the features to trailjournals.com is that readers and follow-ers can send a message via the guest book. Well, after posting what I'd written about Simpson and his snoring, I received a guest book entry.

Monday, March 20, 2017

Hey Whistler,

It's Simpson. Thought your journal was hilarious! Had a great time talking to you, but I must tell you that it was the gentleman next to me against the wall who was snoring so loudly. I hardly slept a wink that night. I made it to Fontana Dam Visitor Center by four o'clock Sunday afternoon. The hike was incredible, and I can't wait to knock off another section. Anyway, thanks again for your company, and I wish you the very best! Will be sure to follow your progress, and best of luck in your journeys! Stay in touch.

Oops! I guess I might have been found guilty in court after all. My deepest apologies, Simpson.

DAY 16

IT'S MY JOB; IT'S WHAT I DO

13.4 Miles Hiked; 210.4 Miles Total
Start: Double Spring Gap Shelter; End: Icewater Spring Shelter

Whistler on the Observation Deck at Clingmans Dome.

Hiking each day for eight to nine hours is almost like having a job. You wake up early, get dressed, take care of personal stuff, eat breakfast, pack your stuff, and walk to work. You'll get a lunch break, stop walking when your shift is over, eat dinner, get ready for bed, sleep, wake up—repeat. It's my job. It's what I do.

My sixteenth day of hiking took me to the prized summit of Clingmans Dome. It was a beautiful morning, with clear skies (although it clouded a bit just as I arrived). The observation tower seemed a bit out of place, but I had to remind myself that it had been built for the multitudes. The views are just out of this world. It's no wonder that the Great Smoky Mountains National Park is the most visited park in the United States.

The descent from Clingmans Dome was horrifying. The ice on the backside of the mountain was heavy and difficult to negotiate, and I slipped and fell three times. The rest of the day's hike was a pleasure, and the trail took me through a beautiful, lush forest of Fraser firs and red spruces. It amazed me how much the forest progressively changed with the differences in elevation.

I haven't yet mentioned the young man who I'd been leapfrogging the previous few days. His name is Quinn, and he had been going by the trail name, "The Mighty Quinn," which he didn't much care for, and was hoping for a new one. Well, Quinn would start his day long after me and inevitably pass me before lunch. So I offered up a new trail name—"Wheels"—that he loved. Unfortunately, Wheels took a shuttle into Gatlinburg that day, and got off the trail for personal reasons, which was a shame, as he was a great young man and a really strong hiker. Perhaps there will be another season for Wheels.

A highlight of the day was when I arrived at Newfound Gap, US 441. The parking lot was packed, and it was actually a bit of a shock after the isolation of the trail. I was standing with a group of thru-hikers when a woman walked up to me and said, "You look like you could use a beer." Did it show that much? Was it that obvious? Anyway, thank you, Heather, trail angel. You made what was already a great day, greater!

That day I hiked with three guys named Hook-set, Strider, and Ho Chi Minh, all great guys about my age, who hiked at around my same speed. The following day's weather called for rain, but that was no surprise—no rain, no Maine!

DAY 17

I'M A LIGHT SLEEPER, BUT REALLY?

12.1 Miles Hiked; 222.5 Miles Total
Start: Icewater Spring Shelter; End: Tricorner Knob Shelter

The previous night, I was in my sleeping bag by eight in anticipation of a good night's sleep. I'd gotten a pretty good idea that it might not go well, when I encountered one of the most ornery people I had ever met. Just prior to our "hiker midnight", Tank made a public announcement and said that he had sleep apnea, that it was a disability and we all needed to "suck it up." He went on to say that if anyone touched him to try to stop his snoring, he would kick them in the face (ouch). Hmmm, how do you even begin to respond to that? Well, unfortunately, Tank wasn't the only one snoring that night. It sounded like a herd of wild animals in that shelter. I tried everything I could to get to sleep—and forget earplugs, as they were totally ineffective.

It was four thirty in the morning when I finally gave up. I got myself dressed, ate breakfast, and packed my backpack. I was hiking with my headlamp by six. I slipped hard on an ice patch, hurt my hip when I landed, and bent a trekking pole. The problem was that I was exhausted—I mean, walking-zombie exhausted. I finally made my way to Pecks Corner Shelter, where a volunteer named Ox was doing shelter maintenance. I explained my situation, that I'd had no sleep the night before, and asked him if, after I had lunch, I could get an hour-long nap (meaning, could he go work elsewhere so it would be quiet). Ox took care of me. He did some work away from the shelter, and gave me my wake-up call at noon.

After waking up, I felt much better, and hiked an additional five miles to Tricorner Knob Shelter, where I set up my tent. One of the rangers could have come by and sited me with a fine, and I would have gladly paid it. I wasn't sleeping in a shelter again. FYI, even though the weather reports had called for rain all day, it never happened! In fact, that day was probably the best weather I'd had thus far.

On another note, something had happened to me a while back that I later gave a lot of thought to:

At Levelland Mountain, I came up behind an older couple, along with who I thought must have been their granddaughter. They were moving quite slowly, when they made an abrupt stop and announced, "This is a good place for lunch." I went around them and wished them a good day.

As I walked away, I thought to myself that they would never make it. Five miles later, I was ready to drop from tiredness, but I hiked that 1.2 miles to Whitley Gap Shelter. The next morning, I'd been hiking along for several miles when I came across them again. They were eating breakfast and we waved at each other. They had actually hiked further than I had. I realized then that the AT is a true equalizer, and it's impossible to know another person's abilities.

DAY 18

OUT OF THE SMOKIES

18.4 Miles Hiked; 240.9 Miles Total
Start: Tricorner Knob Shelter; End: Standing Bear Farm Hostel

My Tree House at Standing Bear Farm.

After hiking with having had limited sleep the night before, I'd found my way to Tricorner Knob Shelter. As soon as I'd arrived, I found what had to be the only tentsite there. I arrived early, and set up my tent, even though the shelter wasn't full—and the rule was that you had to stay in the shelter unless it was full. As I said previously, I was not going to stay in a shelter again unless my life depended on it.

I found myself in my sleeping bag at seven o'clock that evening, and was soon sound asleep. A couple hours later around nine thirty, a light show, along with accompanying thunder, made a grand spectacle. Funny how snoring had kept me awake all night, but how easy it was to sleep through a thunderstorm. I was awake by five in the morning, had breakfast (strawberry frosted Pop-Tarts), took the tent down and packed up, and was on the trail by a quarter to seven (made possible with my trusty headlamp).

I felt superhuman that morning after getting a great night's sleep, and with the benefit of a lot of down hills, I made quick time of it. I did the 18.4 miles in just under seven hours. I arrived at Standing Bear Farm in the early afternoon, and had intended to resupply there and then hike on, but I fell in love with the place and decided to make their tree house my evening accommodation. They offer hot showers, and laundry facilities were included in the price (thirty dollars). They also have a resupply store that easily met my needs until I later arrived at the town of Hot Springs.

I enjoyed a great dinner of pepperoni pizza and the company of three hikers, "Hummingbird," "Engine and Caboose," and "Scoutmaster," along with Scoutmaster's service dog, Scout.

There were two highlights of the day, and the first one was when I met four members of the Carolina Mountain Club. Just as I passed Davenport and as I exited The Great Smoky Mountains National Park, I ran into four guys doing trail maintenance. It's these fine people that have such a passion for the AT, and are partly responsible for making my hike possible. The Carolina Mountain Club and its members maintain ninety-three miles of the AT. The second highlight: That was the day when I had officially completed one tenth of the trail.

DAY 19

YOU'VE GOTTA MAKE HAY WHILE THE SUN SHINES

20 Miles Hiked; 260.9 Miles Total
Start: Standing Bear Farm Hostel; End: Walnut Mountain Shelter

Whistler at the Summit of Max Patch Bald.

I went to bed at eight o'clock the night before, to the sound of a babbling brook directly below my tree house bunk.

Ten hours later, I jumped out of bed when I saw it was already six in the morning. It was time to get ready for work. By the time I had everything packed, had had breakfast and coffee, and paid my bill, it was eighty thirty. My plan was to do between twelve and fifteen miles, but I felt so strong from the rest I'd gotten that I ended up hiking exactly twenty miles. How fortuitous that the distance from Standing Bear Farm to Walnut Mountain Shelter is exactly twenty miles.

I was officially a twenty-miler. Another milestone for me that day was that I had now passed 250 miles of hiking. The weather very much contributed to my ability to put down those miles, as well as the elevations and terrain. So like they say, you've gotta make hay while the sun shines.

One highlight of the day was hiking through Snowbird Bald. I took a picture and texted my sons, as I have fond memories of the time the three of us had hiked there years ago. I recalled how we'd sat on the bald and picked and ate our fill of wild strawberries. Another highlight, hiking Max Patch Bald. The 360-degree views are breathtaking. The next day's hike would take me right through the hiker-friendly town of Hot Springs. When I say "right through," I mean literally, *right through*. The AT goes directly through the middle of their little town, but more about Hot Springs later.

DAY 20

WHY WE HIKE

21.5 Miles Hiked; 282.4 Miles Total
Start: Walnut Mountain Shelter; End: Stealth Camp, Rich Mountain

Having Just Arrived at Hot Springs.

That day started like those before it: early to rise, early to the trail. I walked away from the Walnut Mountain Shelter at seven thirty in the morning, and had the 13.1 miles to Hot Springs checked off before half past noon.

As soon as I left the trail and stepped on the street, a gentleman pulled up and asked if I'd like for him to take my picture. He had apparently seen my attempt to take a selfie with the AT and the sign for Hot Springs in the background. I thanked Bob, and in the same breath, asked him where I could get a fat hamburger. I was directed to the Smoky Mountain Diner. After one huge burger, a large order of fries, and two gigantic cups of Pepsi, I found myself shopping the Dollar General for my resupply.

I stopped in at the local outfitters (Bluff Mountain Outfitters) for a fuel canister and power bars. I happened to notice a pub across the street and thought it would be a great place to re-pack my backpack and enjoy a cold beverage. I had originally planned to stay at Elmer's Sunnybank Inn, but they were fully booked. That was fine, though, because I decided it was too nice a day to quit hiking, so I didn't pursue accommodations elsewhere. I decided to make more hay.

I hadn't planned on hiking very far, but it just seemed to happen. Before I knew it, I'd hiked another seven or so miles. I guess the full belly allowed me to march on while deep in thought. As I hiked onward, I started wondering why "we" hike. There are those who hike for the social aspect to it. I've seen so many hikers who would never consider hiking by themselves, and require others to always be around. Perhaps that's out of a need for a sense of security, or possibly a method to help with holding themselves accountable to finishing the miles they know they have to put down. Then there are others, myself included, who love the solitude, the peacefulness, and the personal freedom that solitary hiking provides.

A point to ponder: There is something special about hearing a bird sing its preassigned song. It's the familiarity and comfort that comes with knowing each bird must whistle their tune—no choice, no repertoire. It's just who they are.

Day 21

WHY IS IT SO EASY TO TALK WITH ANOTHER THRU-HIKER?

13.4 Miles Hiked; 295.8 Miles Total
Start: Stealth Camp, Rich Mountain; End: Stealth Camp, Jones Meadow

One of the Trail's Many Blowdowns.

It was another beautiful hiking day on the Appalachian Trail, with a bit of a late start, though, due to the extra hiking I'd done the night before. The campsite I selected was perfect. It's funny how you search for the perfect site, and will hike later and further just to be certain that you found "it"—even though all you're going to do is get in your tent and go to sleep. Perhaps it's the challenge of the hunt?

It had been a good day to stop and chat with other hikers. Sometimes you are on a mission, and believe it or not, you just don't have time to talk. It might be that you need to get into town for resupply, or that you know you have to lay down some miles and can't stop to talk. In any case, I found myself chatting with several people that day. Some were individuals on day hikes, some were section hikers, while others were thru-hikers like myself. It's always so easy to talk to them. It must be because of our common interest.

Day hikers and section hikers all ask the same questions. They long for the day that they themselves will take their own journey. Other thru-hikers want to know where you started that day, how many miles you will do that day, and where you plan to end your day. Hikers don't talk about current events or politics. One may try, but all they get is an eye roll, and left alone to talk to themselves. In fact, one hiker openly reminded his wife that they agreed to no politics on the trail.

We talk about how many calories are in what we're eating. We talk about the next water source, or what the most recent weather report looks like. The twenty-four-hour news cycle isn't front and center with a thru-hiker; trying to figure out how to consume five thousand or more calories so you can hike another day is the priority. It's what we have in common that makes it so easy to talk with another hiker.

One final thought for the day involves the story of Lou. While hiking, I thought back to a time when one of my sons and I had been section hiking the AT with a dear friend. His name is Lou. Lou is one of the finest gentlemen I've ever met, and have had the pleasure of knowing. At the time, I would have been in my late thirties or early forties, while Lou was my senior by twenty-plus years. He was a very strong hiker, and we would struggle to keep up with him. Lou was soft-spoken, kind, considerate, and was someone who was easy to respect and admire.

Well, one day we had stopped hiking for a moment, and Lou had walked over to where another hiker was sitting. Lou looked in the same direction as this other hiker, who remained seated, and Lou simply remarked how peaceful it was. Without skipping a beat, the other hiker looked up at him and curtly said, "It *was*." In other words, he was making it clear that Lou had interfered and interrupted his peaceful day. Lou, being the gentleman he is, gracefully stepped away.

I share this story, because that hiker missed out on meeting Lou. That hiker's life would have been enriched, and far better off, if he would have stood up, introduced himself, and made time for Lou. If he had, his day would have improved tenfold. I promise you, Lou would have done the same if the roles had been reversed. Isn't it time to *make time* for one another?

DAY 22

LISTEN TO THOSE MOUNTAINS—THEY HAVE STORIES TO TELL

20.6 Miles Hiked; 316.4 Miles Total
Start: Stealth Camp, Jones Meadow; End: Hogback Ridge Shelter

The Shelton Brothers' Gravesite.

I woke up that morning at five thirty, sat up, and thought that I should start my day. I got dressed and walked over and pulled down my food bag from my bear line. As I fixed breakfast, I started feeling rain, so I quickly finished packing and took down my tent. I got my rain gear on, and was hiking by a quarter past seven. I guess I was making hay when the sun didn't shine.

Red Ranger, a fellow hiker, and I had met over lunch at the Smoky Mountain Diner two days prior, and we'd ended up camping together that previous night. He was up shortly after me, skipped breakfast, and packed up just before the rain, as well. We hiked together all day, which was good to help set a pace that may not have been achieved otherwise.

I observed the presence of a number of graves and memorials on and along the trail. There are simple markers, such as the pair of boots I saw tied to a cross the day before, or the beautiful, bronze plaque I'd seen mounted to the face of a large boulder. One grave that I had to walk a side trail to see is the gravesite of the Shelton Brothers. They were two Union soldiers who were killed on that very spot while visiting family in the Confederacy during the Civil War. This trail we walk is rich in history. I would say, "If it could talk . . ."—but in a way, it *does* talk. It talks to us every day. We just need to learn to listen.

DAY 23

SPEAKING OF LISTENING

20.7 Miles Hiked; 337.1 Miles Total
Start: Hogback Ridge Shelter; End: No Business Knob Shelter

Hike Your Own Hike.

It had been another great day for hiking. Elevations were modest, which made for some good miles. In just nine hours, I'd done 20.7 miles of actual hiking. The views were spectacular, on what was a mostly clear day, although there was a quick afternoon shower. I was still going back and forth between North Carolina and Tennessee every day as I hiked. The trail is such that you literally have one foot in North Carolina while the other is in Tennessee, and in another 130 miles I would actually be entering Virginia.

There is a common saying on the trail by which we thru-hikers live. It's referred to as "HYOH"—or "hike your own hike." For example, I'd had a choice the day before while hiking Big Firescald Knob to either take the white-blazed ridge trail, or take what's called a bypass/bad-weather blue-blazed trail. Both sections had a distance of 1.5 miles, but the white-blazed trail runs the top ridge of the mountain, is very rocky, and at times requires hand-over-fist climbs. The blue-blazed trail is rated "easy." Well, I committed to myself that I wasn't going to miss a single white blaze. Though others might have taken the blue-blazed trail, I pass zero judgement. They *hike their own hike*.

Back to the subject of listening: There have been several occasions when a southbound day hiker, or even a faster-than-me northbound thru-hiker, passes me. I'll always give a big smile and greet them. I might get a smile in return, but that's it. It's not until they actually pass me that I realize they have ear-buds stuck in their ears, and haven't heard a single word I said.

There I am, listening to the birds, the water rushing in a stream, to a flock of fifteen to twenty turkeys, two trees rubbing against each other in a stiff breeze, or just listening to the wind, while those other hikers are listening to music. It may just be me, but that's not what I believe the journey is all about—on the other hand, HYOH.

DAY 24

SURE DID MISS THAT MORNING CUP OF JOE

6.1 Miles Hiked; 343.2 Miles Total
Start: No Business Knob Shelter; End: Uncle Johnny's Nolichucky Hostel

Uncle Johnny's Nolichucky Hostel.

The previous night it had stormed like there was no tomorrow, with heavy rain and intense thunder and lightning. Two trees had come down with a huge crack that almost had me out of my tent and into the over-crowded shelter. For a shelter named "No Business Shelter," there was plenty of bad business last night. When morning had finally arrived, I made my oatmeal in my mug and had planned on then making my coffee in said mug immediately after (my method of cleaning my mug . . . it's a hiker thing). Well, I'd only had enough water to fill my mug halfway, and the water source was two-tenths of a mile south on the trail, so I put the water in my jet boil cook stove and poured the hot liquid into my mug, used it to clean my mug, and then drank it—oatmeal tea. Yum.

That day's hike was an easy 6.1 miles to Uncle Johnny's Nolichucky Hostel. When I arrived to check in, I asked for my mail. It was like Christmas when they came out with three boxes. Thank you Susan, Patti, and Gordon for the treats. It's difficult to describe what it means to receive a package from friends and family.

A look behind the scenes of a thru-hike: During the hike, I had to deal with some issues I was having with certain items I'd purchased from Recreational Equipment, Inc.(REI) (Annie, thank you for your help). My hydration system, which is manufactured by Osprey, has a plastic tab that allows it to be hung/suspended in my backpack, which also happens to be made by Osprey). Well, this tab broke the first week I was on the trail, and obviously needed to be replaced. I also had a pair of REI rain pants that had the elastic drawstring break. Annie called to have replacements mailed to Uncle Johnny's Nolichucky Hostel for me.

The person she spoke to said I would have to be the one to call, since I was the customer. That would have been difficult, at best, since I was in the middle of *nowhere*. The person then informed Annie that I could carry the old defective items with me and mail them back once I got home. Really?! Carry two pieces of failed equipment two thousand miles?

Anyway, my REI package was not there when I arrived at the hostel. I attempted to call them, but got disconnected three times. Why was I being disconnected? Because I was in the middle of *nowhere*. Each time I'd call REI, I'd get a different person. I'd have to give them my name, address, zip code, first child's name, and political party affiliation (okay, I'm exaggerating a bit; they didn't ask for my zip code). We did finally determine that they had mailed my package to the Erwin post office. Why would they do this when Annie had given them the hostel's address? It remains a mystery.

So I could either walk (which I'd been doing plenty of lately) to the post office, which was over an hour away on foot, or hitch a ride. Well, as luck would have it, one of Uncle Johnny's associates, Jed was getting ready to make a run to the dump. All I would have to do was help load the garbage. Jed, being a good guy, took me to the post office, where my REI order was waiting. The funny thing, the new hydration system was exactly the same except for the hang tab, which they redesigned completely. Hmmm. Had this been a problem for others? I was going to launder those rain paints before I mailed them back, but based on what I'd had to go through, I was due some satisfaction.

I hope they enjoyed opening that Priority Mail envelope with a special delivery of pants that had spent three weeks soaked in rain and mud and lots of sweat from yours truly.

DAY 25

IF YOU HAVE AN ITCH, SCRATCH IT

19.3 Miles Hiked; 362.5 Miles Total
Start: Uncle Johnny's Nolichucky Hostel; End: 0.8 miles from Iron Mountain Gap

The Spruce Forest on Unaka Mountain.

I had already decided the night before that I wouldn't be taking the morning shuttle the hostel offered to breakfast. The shuttle didn't leave until eight thirty, and I had already planned to be back on the trail by then. Red Ranger also decided against the shuttle, but for a different reason. He had made arrangements to hire someone to drive him to Iron Mountain Gap, twenty miles north, so he could slack pack back to Uncle Johnny's. For those of you who don't know, "slack packing" is when you take a day pack with food (i.e., lunch and snacks) and water, catch a shuttle further up the trail, and hike your way back, the benefit being the light pack and ease of the hike. The miles still count. Remember, *HYOH*.

I ran into Red Ranger at Indian Grave Gap at lunchtime, while he was heading south and I was continuing north. He had hiked twelve miles and I had hiked only eight miles. He looked fresh and light on his feet; I looked like I needed a shower and a blood transfusion.

The hike that day started at about 1,800 feet, and went up to just over five thousand feet. The transitional changes in the landscape are unmistakable. The lower elevations boast mature hardwoods, with mountain laurel and some conifers. The hike took me to a beautiful, dense spruce forest at more than five thousand feet up Unaka Mountain. The difference was remarkable, in that it was so clearly delineated. The spruce forest was so dense that if you threw a stone, you couldn't help but hit a tree. The forest floor was thick in seasonally shed needles, which made for a soft, almost carpet-like, feel underfoot—a vast difference from the sharp, rocky tread normally felt on the trail.

The sun made its way through the thick canopy in beams of light that almost seemed to mimic Hollywood special effects. If not for the stark, white blazes on the dark trunks of select trees, finding the way/trail would have been impossible. As I walked, I imagined that if there were such a thing as elves, hobbits, and fairies, surely this was where they would live. These huge, majestic spruce trees stood tall over their young. The immature trees lined up in almost perfect formation and shape. It was like I was walking through a Christmas tree farm, with every tree a perfect choice to take home.

A little hiking advice: While hiking, if your bootlaces aren't feeling right, re-tie them. If there is something in your backpack rattling, take your pack off, find the culprit, and stop the rattling. If you have your clothes layered and you're hot, stop hiking, take off that layer(s), and restart your hike. In other words, if you have an itch, scratch it. Trust me, it makes for a much more enjoyable hike.

DAY 26

AND IT HUFFED AND IT PUFFED

20.5 Miles Hiked; 383 Miles Total
Start: 8 miles from Iron Mountain Gap; End: Stan Murray Shelter

The Rootapus Snakeopotamus.

I woke early this morning and was on the trail by a quarter past seven. I arrived at Iron Mountain Gap just before eight o'clock, and hoped to meet Red Ranger as he got dropped off by Uncle Johnny's shuttle. I waited a few minutes and never saw him, so I hiked on. It was one of those days where you hike all day and practically never see another soul. I saw several day hikers but they were all southbound. No north-bound ("NoBo") hikers at all but for myself. I stopped at Hughes Gap for lunch, ate quickly, packed up, and hiked on.

Shortly after, the weather really got strange. The air got super cold and the sky turned dark. The temperature must have dropped twenty degrees in a matter of minutes. There I was, hiking in shorts and a T-shirt, and starting to shiver. I dropped my pack and pulled out my rain gear just as it started to rain. I continued to hike, and started to warm up from the activity. I was actually making good time and mile-age, so I decided to skip the next shelter and keep moving.

At one point I was at Jane Bald, and the wind was blowing so hard that it blew me off my feet. I got up and it took all I had to walk into the wind without getting blown to the ground again. I finally got to Stan Murray Shelter, where I was the only person there. I set my tent up in the shelter, and hoped and prayed that no one else showed. If they did, I was going to have to move my tent outside.

While hiking, there are several potentially dangerous things to look out for that do not get the attention they deserve. I'll cover one of these hazards now. This creature lurks on the trail in the most stealth-iest of ways. An unsuspecting hiker is certain to be caught by surprise. The "Rootapus Snakeopotamus" (my Latin name for them) lays about the trail waiting for some poor unsuspecting hiker to step over them. Their method of attack is to reach up, grab your boot, and attempt to trip you and bring you down. Tired hikers are more likely to be tripped up by them, so you must always be on alert. They are very clever, and at times will hide their whereabouts under the fallen leaves. They resemble tree roots, and will actually anchor themselves to the ground, but don't be fooled by these very dangerous creatures. Step high, my friends, and keep those boots out of reach.

For the record, tree roots are not out to get us. The surface roots I jokingly wrote about here are just doing the best they can to survive in places where the soil has eroded which is keeping them from getting the soil oxygen and nutrients needed for the health of the tree.

DAY 27

THE PATH OF LEAST RESISTANCE

20.7 Miles Hiked; 403.7 Miles Total
Start: Stan Murray Shelter; End: Stealth Camp, Slide Hollow

A River Runs through It—the Trail, That Is.

Pitching my tent in the shelter turned out to have been a stroke of genius, as it ended up working out really well for me that night. The storm was one that I didn't want to be sleeping out under those big trees for fear of a widow-maker that might have come crashing through my tent. The trail was littered with huge branches and tree blowdowns, which was a true indication of just how severe this storm had been.

It was still raining when I awoke, so I got a bit of a late start. I decided that I would hike the 1.9 miles to the Overmountain Shelter for my morning coffee and breakfast. Overmountain is a unique shelter that was repurposed from an old barn. I arrived right at eighty thirty, and talked with a couple of thru-hikers, who told me the shelter had been packed the night before. That made me really happy with my decision to stay at Stan Murray Shelter (not that my feet could have gone any further, anyway).

The sun was just breaking through the clouds, which provided the view Overmountain Shelter is known for having. It was kind of funny how a group of us took in the view. We were just staring at the mountains like a high-action movie was playing before us. No action; just the amazing beauty of rolling hills in the forefront, and tall, majestic mountains as the backdrop. It was one of those "pinch-me" moments I knew I'd always remember as it was etching itself in my mind for future reflection.

After my breakfast, I packed up and hit the trail—or should I say, the river. All that rain water had to go somewhere, so why not have that be the trail? The trail had been the path of least resistance for all that water, and unfortunately, that was the same trail we all had to trek. At times the water was up to my ankles and spilling into my boots; where it was shallow was like hiking in pudding.

The Roan Highlands are known for both the difficulty of the hike, and for the views they afford. Well, a heavy fog provided cover for the views, but the hiking difficulties remained. The highlight of the day was passing the sign that informed me I'd officially left North Carolina safely behind me. Two states down, twelve to go.

DAY 28

FREE MILES? SURE, I'LL TAKE SOME OF THOSE

15.2 Miles Hiked; 418.9 Miles Total
Start: Stealth Camp, Slide Hollow; End: Kincora Hiking Hostel

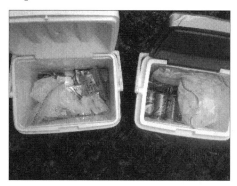

Trail Magic Left by Stanley the Dog.

That day's hiking entailed what I'm going to call a "free miles day". In other words, an easy hike; limited climbs and easy downs. I did the fifteen-plus miles in six hours of stress-free hiking. I had the pleasure of hiking a couple of those hours with Mr. T. Mr. T and I were close in age, hiked at the same pace, and we had great conversation. We split just as I was getting ready to stop by Kincora Hiking Hostel to pick up a package my sister had sent me. I hadn't actually planned on staying at the hostel, but quickly changed my mind once I arrived.

Bob Peoples is the owner and operator, and is a legend of the Appalachian Trail. His warm welcome convinced me to stay (that, and his twelve cats). The deal there is that a person can stay for a recommended donation of five dollars. The hostel's common area includes a full kitchen for hikers' use. Showers, laundry facility, bathrooms, and a shuttle to local restaurants and an Ingles grocery store are also available. This is a not-for-profit hostel, so don't expect the Hilton.

The Kincora Hostel is located near Hampton, Tennessee, just a short trek off the trail. By all appearances, it's not much to look at, and you might consider skipping it. Honestly, it's old, run down, and smells like old socks—but you have to stay here. Kincora is legendary, and the man behind Kincora, Bob Peoples, is known as a superhero of the Appalachian Trail. At seventy-plus years old, he has devoted his life to trail maintenance, trail building, and shelter building, and has hosted well over twenty thousand hikers at his hostel. Since 1988, he has logged an average of over three hundred volunteer hours on the trail each year. Do yourself a huge favor, and immerse yourself in a true part of hiker history and culture: *Stay at the Kincora*. When you do, shake this man's hand and thank him for helping make your hike possible.

I also had the pleasure of meeting Stanley the dog that day. As I was hiking, Stanley and his owner (I have no idea what his owner's name is) were both hiking south. Stanley was a lab, Irish-setter mix with the sweetest disposition. Anyway, when I had finished loving on Stanley, I continued on with my hike, only to find two coolers full of trail magic. A note on top of the coolers welcomed hikers to enjoy their contents— yep, you guessed it—the note was signed and left for thru-hikers by Stanley the dog.

Day 29

SOMETIMES YOU GOTTA GO DOWN BEFORE YOU CAN GO UP

17.6 Miles Hiked; 436.5 Miles Total
Start: Kincora Hiking Hostel; End: Vandeventer Shelter

Laurel Fork Falls.

I left Kincora Hostel that morning at a quarter past seven, but not empty-handed. Bob Peoples, the proprietor, sliced off four huge pieces of banana nut bread for me to take on the trail. It was consumed long before I made it back to the trailhead. I had ended up being the only hiker at the hostel the night before, which made for a very quiet night. Boots (an orange tabby cat) kept me company as he slept with me all night.

The start of my day's hike was unique, in that the rock formations I climbed were like huge blocks stacked on top of one another. It amazed me how much the physical makeup of one mountain differs from the next. That mountain (Pond Mountain) looked as though fine stone masons had erected it stone by stone, carefully cutting and fitting each one in a specific, predetermined location. Like those masons who built the great cathedrals and pyramids, this mountain, in its own free-form shape, was designed and built by a greater power, each stone placed exactly where He planned.

The hike started with a huge descent over a boulder field, and the deeper I descended, the louder the roaring of Laurel Fork Falls became. When the Falls finally came into view, I found myself moving in slow motion, as it was totally mesmerizing. Laurel Falls was worth the price of admission—that huge descent. That "ticket" provided a front-row seat, with an audience of one for the big show.

Well, sometimes you have to go down before you can go up. Reality hit soon after I started my hike away from the falls. Pond Mountain had asked for full payment for that show, the cost of which, was 3,800 feet. It was brutal, but still worth it. My hike the next day looked to be a lot easier, with limited elevation changes, so I was hoping to put down some big miles that day. If I did, it would make the next day, Tuesday, a short one, and would take me into Damascus. I though I might actually take that Wednesday off, too, and it would be my first zero day after hiking nonstop for a full month. I was tired!

DAY 30

RUINS OF THE PEOPLE OF APPALACHIA

24.8 Miles Hiked; 461.3 Miles Total
Start: Vandeventer Shelter; End: Stealth Camp

One of Many Ruins along the Trail.

Before I get into this day's hike, I want to take you back to my hike the day before. I realized that I left out a big portion of that day's adventures. Once I'd come to US 321, I stopped at Shook Branch Recreation Area, which is an area with picnic facilities and a sandy beach. It had been the perfect spot for me to sit at a table and enjoy my lunch. The whole time, I imagined how perfect it would have been if there had been a Coke machine there.

After I'd finished my lunch, I started hiking again where the trail takes you along the shoreline of Watauga Lake. In fact, the trail follows this man-made, dammed lake for a couple of miles. You continue until you cross over the Watauga Dam, follow the road that is sparsely blazed, and then get back on the trail for a big ascent. The higher I'd gone, the bigger my view had gotten of the lake, which was breathtakingly beautiful. Higher still, and I could see the marina across the lake.

My imagination ran away with me as I continued to think about that Coke machine. That marina had to have been ten miles away, and I still kept thinking how great it would have been to mosey on over there for an ice-cold drink. My imagination didn't stop there. I imagined walking up to those blue canopies and finding a dockside bar. I would sit down and people would ask if I was an AT thru-hiker. I'd respond that yes, I was, and I would tell them all about my adventures after I ordered myself a cold drink. "No, Whistler," they would all say, "your money's no good here. We're buying your drinks today." I'd say, "Well, in that case, I'll have the big-slurp, bottomless mug of ice-cold beer. Once that beer arrives, I'll wet my whistle and tell you all my stories."

So back to the following day's hike: It rained almost all day, I got soaked, my feet turned into prunes, I hiked 24.8 miles—the end.

I do want to talk about the ruins that one sees as you hike the AT. It's not uncommon to come across an old stone foundation, or to find a fully intact stone fireplace, in the middle of nowhere. These are the remnants of a time when the people of Appalachia lived and worked in these mountains. There is a long history of the government's involvement in "assisting" the people of Appalachia. Job creation, education, the introduction of jobs in the coal mines, the building of dams for cheap electricity, and actually relocating people to remove them from poverty. A lot of falsehoods, myths, and distortions were promoted to support those acts. Later studies and published papers dispelled those stereotypes, but they unfortunately still follow the people of Appalachia today.

DAY 31

IS THIS PLACE (DAMASCUS) FOR REAL?

8.3 Miles Hiked; 469.6 Miles Total
Start: Stealth Camp; End: Damascus, Virginia

Crossing from Tennessee into Virginia.

The day before, I had actually planned on stopping and staying at Double Spring Gap Shelter, but it was full. Two hikers, Onion and Floater, were about to make room, but I thought I'd go on a couple more miles, as I still had some steam in my legs. Besides, as you know, I'm not really into sleeping in shelters. It had been raining all day, and as I turned to start back on the trail, the sun made its first appearance of the day. I took that as a sign, and marched on. I found the perfect stealth campsite, just over two miles further north, and yes, two miles closer to Damascus. I took that as another sign.

The town of Damascus, Virginia is located along the southern border of Virginia, in Washington County. The population of under nine hundred explodes during the annual Trail Days Festival, when over twenty thousand visitors and hikers make their way to this quaint little town. The Trail Days Festival is also known to be the largest single gathering of Appalachian Trail hikers anywhere. The town itself is commonly referred to as "Trail Town, USA" because of the four scenic trails that all converge there. The Appalachian Trail, US Bicycle Route 76, the Iron Mountain Trail, and the Virginia Creeper Trail make Damascus a hotspot for the active at heart. There are several outfitters in the town, and a good number of bicycle rental shops, which tells you how important visitors are in terms of the contribution they provide to the town's economic stability.

When I woke up in the morning, it was raining, and it was pretty evident that it had done so all night. I started packing what I could while still inside my tent. Do you know that it stopped raining just as I had been thinking about taking down my tent? I took that as yet another sign. I only had 8.3 miles into Damascus, and was already getting excited about my short day and my commitment to taking my first zero day, the day after.

Just three miles or so prior to Damascus, is the Tennessee/Virginia state line. Floater, a fellow hiker, came by just as I was about to take a selfie in front of the sign. She took my picture, and I returned the favor. I took that as, still, another sign. When I eventually came off the trail, I could not believe how beautiful Damascus was—picture perfect in every way. Gardens, landscaping, and the park in the center of town is just beautiful. I took that as a sign.

I walked up the main street and it was there where I bumped into Red Ranger. I took that as a sign. We made plans to meet for lunch after I'd had the opportunity to stop by the post office and local outfitters for my packages from Annie and my daughter-in-law, Lauren. After lunch, I made a minor resupply, got back to the Hikers Inn, and took a shower. The inn took my laundry (those poor people), and then I enjoyed an ice-cold beer. Oh, the sign I mentioned, I think it was also a sign, and it told me that taking a zero the next day was the right thing to do. It was time for a recharge!

Day 32

What One Does When One Takes a Zero

0 Miles Hiked; 469.6 Miles Total
Start: Damascus, Virginia; End: Damascus, Virginia

Mt. Rogers Outfitters, Damascus, Virginia.

I'd been thinking through what I could possibly write about in my journal on that day. There I was, taking my first and oh-so-pleasant zero in the quaint and very hiker friendly town of Damascus, Virginia—so what was there to write about? Well, believe it or not, you actually do plan and work when you take a day off the trail. Sure, there's plenty of downtime to eat and drink, and repeat that throughout the day. But one must resupply, repair, and replace worn and broken equipment, and study the trail guide for the next stops and future resupplies.

For example, the insoles of my boots had worn through after hiking the first nearly five hundred miles, so I picked up a new pair at

Mt. Rogers Outfitters. For the record, I can't recommend Mt. Rogers Outfitters enough. Next, a buckle on one of the straps that I used for cinching my tent to my backpack had broken. The guys at Mt. Rogers Outfitters came up with a fix for my problem, and didn't even charge me. I was then off to the local grocery store, which was about a mile away, for a few odds and ends. My food bag had now been fully stocked for the next hundred miles. I was fully restocked, recharged, and ready to lay down some northbound miles.

The weather report for that evening and the next day called for rain and snow—no more soft living for this hiker.

Day 33

GOODBYE, DAMASCUS; HELLO, APPALACHIAN TRAIL

21.8 Miles Hiked; 491.4 Miles Total
Start: Damascus, Virginia; End: Stealth Camp

What I Woke up To; the Trail Is Somewhere under There.

You would think it would be difficult to leave civilization and all the comforts it has to offer, but it was actually quite easy. The day and a half off the trail did me a lot of good, but to be honest, I'd been bored out of my mind. I am not wired for sitting around. I need to be moving.

After having taken care of my zero-day hiking responsibilities, I watched a couple of movies from my hosts' very extensive library of DVDs. I also made a dinner run to Hey Joe's, a restaurant in Damascus, for another "everything" burrito. I'm really glad I did, as I ran into Fish and Radio, two hikers I'd met at the Nantahala Outdoor Center, whom I had not seen since. I sat with them and we each told our tales. It was a lot of fun to catch up. They are two really great young men who helped restore my confidence in today's youth.

What does that even mean? Well, to be honest, it takes a huge amount of perseverance and drive to do what we were doing. This long-distance hiking had each of us waking up each morning with the full understanding that we were going to meet adversity and challenges that most people would not be prepared for, or willing to accept. My limited experience and time on the trail had already shown me the difference between those who possess this internal drive and those who obviously don't. Fish and Radio had what it took, and if I'd been asked to predict the future of their journey, I would have said they would both summit Mount Katahdin.

I was up that morning at a quarter past five, and had coffee and a 660-calorie cinnamon bun that I'd warmed in the microwave for breakfast (again, it's all about the calories). I was packed and ready, my backpack on, by six thirty, and then I was out the door. I felt really strong all day, and only stopped hiking when the snow and ice got to be just too dangerous to hike in (I hate it when the meteorologists are right).

I did have the pleasure of hiking that afternoon with Onion, who I'd met up with shortly after I had stopped at Saunders Shelter for lunch. It had been a while since our last meeting and I have great admiration for Onion and her hiking partner "Floater". This hike has served to solidify my positive view of today's youth. We hiked to Lost Mountain Shelter together, where she called it a day, but was also waiting for Floater to catch up. It was just after two o'clock, and I'd really hoped to get twenty or more miles in, so I continued on. I finally stopped when I found what had been the only decent stealth campsite I'd seen in a long time, and I knew I had better take it quickly due to the weather.

The next day's big adventure, weather permitting, was going to be seeing the feral ponies at Grayson Highlands State Park. I'd been looking forward to seeing them for as long as I had been planning my entire hike.

Day 34

ALL THE PRETTY LITTLE PONIES

18.2 Miles Hiked; 509.6 Miles Total
Start: Stealth Camp; End: Old Orchard Shelter

Me and My Pony.

The night before had been a nightmare. I'd been in my sleeping bag by six o'clock that evening, in full-on mummified mode. I'd put every piece of clothing on that I had with me: three shirts, a rain jacket, both long and regular underwear, hiking pants, rain pants, socks, gloves, and my toque. The weather was horrible, with winds gusts of forty to fifty miles per hour. Tree limbs could be heard snapping off trees all night. I felt like I was being used for target practice all night, as ice, snow clumps, and small branches came falling out of the trees and onto my tent. I woke every hour on the hour to knock the snow off the tent, fearing it would cave in under the excessive weight.

When that morning arrived, there was five to six inches of snow on the ground. Drifts were knee deep. I was up early, but it took additional time to break camp. I packed my tent, with ice attached that added much unwanted weight to my pack. It was exactly eight o'clock before I was on the trail, with the wind, snow, and ice having made it slow going for sure. My primary goal for the day was to see those ponies at Grayson Highlands State Park.

At Massie Gap, Rhododendron Trail in Grayson Highlands State Park, herds of "introduced" ponies can be found that have roamed free and wild along the grassy balds and spruce forests of Wilburn Ridge for more than forty years. Their thick manes blow in the wind as they graze alongside the trails. The ponies are very accustomed to humans, and rarely halt their grazing as hikers pass close by. Many locals touch and feed the ponies, though this practice is frowned upon and is against park policy. Each year, park officials round up the herd and check for health problems, and whether the herd size needs to be reduced; the excess colts are sold at auction.

I was not only able to see them, I got to pet them and take a few selfies with them, as well. It was so cool! I felt like a small child, in total wonder of those precious creatures, with their curiosity and their obvious desire for a treat—one I was ill-prepared to offer. The absence of the slightest hint of inhibitions or fear of this thru-hiker having entered their world was welcomed, and it was a gift to be able to witness true, absolute trust.

Yet another highlight of that day: I had officially hiked five hundred miles!

DAY 35

THE ATTRACTION OF PIZZA

23.2 Miles Hiked; 532.8 Miles Total
Start: Old Orchard Shelter; End: Partnership Shelter

Thank You, Pizza Hut.

When I arrived at Old Orchard Shelter the night before, I'd found the perfect level site for my tent, with a lush cover of grass. A father, Boon Dog, and daughter, Boots, were already set up and had a great fire going. They were doing a three-day, southbound section of the trail. They invited me to join them by their fire. They didn't need to ask me twice. I fixed my dinner while I enjoyed the warmth of both the fire and their company.

Morning seemed to come quickly, and I knew I had to get up and going. I finally listened to myself at six o'clock. I was on the trail just before eight, with one primary goal/objective in mind. Pizza lay in waiting a short 23.2 miles up the trail—which would ordinarily be a great distance, but it seemed like much shorter with pizza as motivation.

To explain, Partnership Shelter is located right next to the Mount Rogers Welcome Center, and is known as one of two shelters on the AT where you can order and have pizza delivered. I arrived at six thirty that night, and went to the welcome center, where they have a free phone set up along with the menu. I ordered two medium-sized meat lovers' pizzas, and ate one for dinner, while the other I planned to eat for breakfast (I love cold pizza).

Speaking of food (a favorite pastime for long-distance hikers), I realized a phenomenon regarding my food bag. I call it my hate/love relationship with my food bag.

When you are leaving a town after a resupply, your food bag is packed full. You hate the bag because of the additional weight, but you love the bag because it carries all the food you're going to eat for sustenance. As your food bag's contents diminish you love your bag for how light it is, which allows you to hike quickly and puts less strain on your legs, feet, and back—but you hate your food bag for the lack of food it contains within.

As an aside, I didn't see a single hiker all day. Not a NoBo, SoBo, section hiker, or day hiker—no one! I did meet up with Mcflurry and Sequoia, Songbird, and Crispy and Enox at Partnership Shelter once I arrived. This group of "twenty something" year old hikers and I have been leapfrogging for the last couple of days. It's not uncommon to meet groups of hikers like this and once again, this hike is what we all have in common and draws us together.

DAY 36

I SHOULD HAVE KNOWN BETTER

18.3 Miles Hiked; 551.1 Miles Total
Start: Partnership Shelter; End: Reed Creek

Me and My Shadow.

I had thought I'd give the Partnership Shelter a try, instead of setting up my tent. All the hikers there were young, early-to-mid-twenties young. I thought I'd be safe with regard to heavy snoring. I should have known better. It was right at ten thirty that night, after staring at the shelter ceiling for two hours, when I decided to pitch my tent. It took me about five minutes to set it up, and I'm guessing I was asleep by the sixth minute (I probably snored myself to sleep). Truth be told, it's me; I'm a very light sleeper. No fault to those who snore; they are always content.

The snow and rain we'd had just two days ago made for wet socks and boots—the perfect combination for soft and tender feet. My right little piggy had developed a good-sized blister (yep, I stabbed him), while a few of his mates had been thinking about joining the party. Crazy how something so small can make for tough miles.

The weather during the day was what you hike hundreds of miles for; it was perfect. Beautiful, sunny, and warm, but with some cool breezes, too. My objective was to have a short mileage day to allow my dogs the opportunity to recover from the beating they'd been through lately. I had planned on stopping at Davis Path Campsite, but quickly determined that there was no level tentsite there or any water, so backpack was back on, and I hiked an additional four miles. The good news was that I'd gotten four miles further north. The bad news was that my feet were feeling pretty bad. I would see what tomorrow would bring. The human body can be pretty resilient . . . I sure hoped so.

The milestone for the day was that I had now completed a quarter of the journey: 550 miles in five weeks.

WATER

I've seen you come; I've seen you go.
You're rain and sleet and ice and snow.
I'll dread your falling from the sky.
I'll curse your discomfort, is the reason why.
I'll cross you; I'll ford you.
I'll hate and adore you.
I'll run for shelter upon your arrival.
I'll seek and hunt you for my very survival.
You're tasteless and clear,
But you're abundantly dear.
I've seen your ebbs; I've seen your flows—
For you're the reason this forest grows.

(April, 9th, 2017, Day 36)

DAY 37

SERIOUSLY, I'M NOT WHINING

18.7 Miles Hiked; 569.8 Miles Total
Start: Reed Creek; End: Walker Gap

Whistler in Front of Chestnut Knob Shelter.

It was an absolutely beautiful day that day: clear skies, and sunny and warm, with some cool breezes thrown in for good measure. I'd realized while hiking along that morning that maybe I sounded like I was whining in some of what I'd written in my journal entries. Please be assured that my reporting on weather or trail conditions was nothing more than a daily account of what had occurred that day. I was prepared (I sure as heck should have been) to accept whatever the trail threw my way. I'm not going to lie—a good percentage of the time it's miserable. In fact, I would venture to say that any thru-hiker would say it was the most difficult thing they'd ever done, and I, for one, wouldn't have changed one minute of it.

I hiked 17.5 miles that day before I saw anyone. So funny how that can happen. You know there are lots of other crazy fools out there, but you can hike all day and not see another soul. As I was hiking over Chestnut Ridge and toward Chestnut Knob Shelter, I came upon a hiker who was sitting all by himself. I walked over, said hello, and introduced myself as Whistler. Without skipping a beat, he asked me, "How was your pizza?" Having never met this gentleman, my first thought was that perhaps he had been following me online through my journal.

No, as it turned out, his wife had been following my journal, and told her husband to say hello if he met me. His self-appointed trail name was "Now or Never," which was meant to represent his motivation for hiking. After all, none of us were getting any younger, and "Now or Never" represented the truth of why we had taken on this monumental task.

Chestnut Knob Shelter is apparently an old forest warden's home/station that was converted to a shelter for hikers. It is constructed entirely of stone, with four walls and a door, which is very unusual, as most shelters are constructed in the manner of a three-sided "lean-to." I seriously thought about spending the night there (in my tent, of course), but I really needed water, and that shelter did not have a source close by. I would have enjoyed spending more time with Now or Never, and he did try to convince me to stay (I got the impression he was lonely), but the call of fresh cool water won over, so off I went.

It was just another 1.5 miles north where I found the perfect stealth site, and it had a spring of water magically bubbling out of the ground nearby—which meant I could fix myself a cup of tea.

Day 38

WHERE HAVE ALL THE HIKERS GONE?

22.3 Miles Hiked; 592.1 Miles Total
Start: Walker Gap; End: Stealth Camp, Helveys Mill Shelter

Brad and Cornucopia's Van; Georgia to Maine.

What an incredible day I'd had. It had started with me waking up early to perform some doctoring on my feet. It seemed that a couple of toenails had been thinking of abandoning ship. I believe I'd done all I could do in my feeble attempts to save them. I had the toenails taped on at that point, using first aid tape, in the hopes that the nail beds would firm up. Of course, I'd stubbed my boots into some roots and rocks several times along the way—ouch.

It was another day where I saw absolutely no northbound hikers. I saw several day- and section hikers, but not a single northbounder. It was a true mystery. Had they gotten sucked into that gingerbread house out in the middle of the forest by a wicked witch? Were they currently hiker stew? I believed it was due to some sort of unexplained phenomenon, like the Devil's Triangle, or Bigfoot. More importantly, was I next?

It was turkey hunting season, and I crossed paths with two young guys out turkey hunting that morning. They had a lot of questions about my hiking, and the AT in particular, while I had a few questions about turkey hunting. When I asked, they were more than happy to demonstrate their turkey calling skills. I sure was glad I hadn't worn my turkey-feather headdress that morning.

That day, I had manna from heaven come to me (more commonly known as trail magic).

While coming off the trail to cross VA 623, I noticed a couple standing by a van. I said hello and we exchanged the expected pleas-antries. I'm not exactly sure the thing that prompted what happened next, but before I knew it, I had been invited to have something to eat with them. It turned out that the woman was an avid hiker, with a true passion for the AT, having hiked several hundred miles as a section hiker with her husband Brad as her ground support.

She asked me if I would like turkey or ham. I obviously didn't care which, as I would have eaten the tires off their van. The next thing I knew, granola bars and cheese sticks were being forced upon me, and there was little to no resistance on my part. I felt blessed beyond my pea-brained comprehension. When I asked her what her trail name was, she replied that she didn't have one. I offered up the trail name "Cornucopia" as a suggestion, which she happily accepted. Yes, the back of her van was overflowing with a bounty of food and drink, it was obvious to me that her new trail name, Cornucopia, also fit her bountiful spirit.

I hiked on, but as luck would have it, Cornucopia and I later met at the next shelter, and we had lunch together (where I also performed more surgery on my feet . . . how appetizing that must have been for my new friend). After lunch, I hiked on past her, and when I arrived at Suiter Road, Cornucopia's husband Brad was waiting to meet her—and I was again on the receiving end of more trail magic. Juice and popsicles, just what the doctor had ordered.

Several hours later and toward the end of my day, trail magic struck yet again! As I came to US Route 52, I met a thru-hiker named Pigeon Toe, who had completed the trail in 2016. He was just getting ready to pack up his motor home after a long day of having bestowed trail magic on lucky thru-hikers. Pigeon Toe saw me, called me over, and loaded me up. Let's just say, the last 1.5 miles I hiked were the most difficult of the day because of the additional weight from all the food this fine gentleman provided.

And now it's time for some hiking advice; a place for everything, and everything in its place: When thru-hiking, you will save yourself time and aggravation if you put everything in the same place every time. It takes the worrying out of your hiking if you know where everything is. Need your headlamp, no worries; you'll know exactly where it is. Need your toilet paper? You get the idea.

Day 39

JUST AS I WAS GETTING TRULY CONCERNED

20.3 Miles Hiked; 612.4 Miles Total
Start: Stealth Camp, Helveys Mill Shelter; End: Stealth Camp

The Hiker Double Cheeseburger at Trent's.

It started as a day of hiking with no other hikers to be seen. I started to think maybe I had it all wrong. What if I was the subject of a cruel hoax? What if someone had painted white blazes on selected trees and I was going in a huge circle? Maybe the other NoBos were sitting around a campfire each night asking about me: "Hey, what do you suppose ever happened to that hiker from—where was that, again? Oh yeah, Nova Scotia, I think. Where is that, anyway? What was his name again? 'Whittler'? 'Whiskers'? No, no, it was Whistler. That's it. I'm sure. A nice fellow. Handsome, too. Maybe he got caught up in that whole wicked-witch-gingerbread-house thing. You know, he might even be hiker stew by now."

But then it happened: I found a NoBo. I discovered Will-da-Beast just before two o'clock that afternoon. I wasn't alone, after all.

Right after I had my first (light) lunch at Jenny Knob Shelter, I also met Dr. J on the trail. Dr. J was doing a section hike through most of Virginia. We ended up hiking together for about two hours, which was nice to be able to talk and be with someone who hiked at my same pace. I convinced him to join me for lunch (my second lunch), which was going to be at Trent's Grocery Store. Trent's has a solid reputation among hikers for its great double cheeseburger.

I had woken up that morning thinking about that cheeseburger, and it didn't disappoint. I had an order of fries, a bottle of coke, and a big bag of Fritos corn chips. It wasn't until after I'd eaten every bit of all that that I read the calorie count for the Fritos: 160 calories per serving. A "serving" equals twenty-eight chips. Ten servings per bag. That equaled 1,600 calories! Score! I was pretty sure I'd gotten in the suggested number of calories per day for hikers (six thousand)..

It was a relatively easy hike that day, with limited elevation changes and uneventful terrain (my feet appreciated that)—a lot of "puds" (pointless ups and downs), or as my granddaughter Katy Ellis would say, "Pointless uppa downs."

I found a perfect place to set up my tent on a beautiful, open, grassy field. I would have a relatively short day tomorrow, so I thought I would maybe sleep in a bit. I was just about twenty-two miles from Pearisburg, where I planned to take a room. It was *very* much time for a shower and a resupply, to do some laundry, and have some more "town food." I didn't want to get there late, because I wanted to have a full day there.

THE WOOD

How many miles must I walk
Before I feel worthy of our talk?
I've walked amongst you countless days,
My hope, my tribute to pay you praise.
The branches strong, the very best
Providing refuge for your birds to nest.
The roots dig deep with all their might
To grasp and clutch the soil tight.
Poised there soaring to reach for sky,
Their true ambition is the reason why.
The air is pure, the air is clean.
Your thankless purpose that I glean.
And when it's time to fall and go,
Enrich the soil that the young may grow.
The time is now, I know I should,
Praise you Lord for The Wood.

(April, 12th, 2017, Day 39)

DAY 40

WHAT I'VE LEARNED ALONG THE WAY

19.7 Miles Hiked; 632.1 Miles Total
Start: Stealth Camp; End: Pearis Ledges

Pearis Ledges; View from My Tent Tonight.

Having planned a later start, I didn't get up until seven that morning. I had a big breakfast, which consisted of two packages of oatmeal and a pack of Pop-Tarts with my coffee.

I took it slow and easy, knowing that I didn't have far to go and that I'd be spending the following day in Pearisburg. I had it all planned out: Hardee's for breakfast, Lucky Star Chinese (all you can eat) for lunch, Pizza Hut for dinner, and Dairy Queen for dessert. In between my planned meals, there would be a shower—*showers*, perhaps maybe three or four—laundry, shopping/resupply, and a visit to the post office.

While hiking, I thought about some of the things I'd learned that I would now like to pass along:

1. Bears do not poop in the woods. They poop on the trail.

2. If you meet another thru-hiker and ask them their trail name, if they tell you theirs but don't ask for yours, put your pack back on and keep hiking. If you stay, you will end up having a conversation with one of the latest of a generation of hiking narcissists. They will let you know how great they are and how blessed you are to be in their presence. Thankfully, I have also met many of that same generation whose mommas brought them up right.

3. Trail angels love giving as much as, or perhaps enjoy it more than, hikers enjoy receiving trail magic.

4. Trail angels *really are* angels.

5. Store-brand Pop-Tarts taste exactly like the Kellogg's brand, and they cost far less.

6. Flavor your water; you'll drink a lot more if you do.

7. Sit down whenever you get the chance.

8. If you hear drumming while you're hiking, the natives are not restless. You are hearing the sound of a male grouse thumping/beating its wings. It's what they do to impress the chicks.

Look forward to more advice; it'll come later, just as I continued to learn those lessons along the way.

DAY 41

WHAT'S THAT YOU SAY? YOU WANT TO KNOW WHAT A THRU-HIKER EATS?

1.5 Miles Hiked; 633.6 Miles Total
Start: Pearis Ledges; End: Plaza Motel, Pearisburg, Virginia

An Average Day's Menu for a Thru-Hiker.

Before I get into what a thru-hiker eats, I feel compelled to share this: It appeared that as of late, the Appalachian Trail Garden Club had been working evenings as I slept. Beautiful wild flowers had arrived, seemingly as though secret gardeners had worked through the night to provide a gift of Spring color for the thru-hikers. Trilliums, wild violet, dogwoods, and bloodroot abounded, as though on a secret schedule that only they knew; others would arrive based on a later, less-rushed timeline, another future blessing for us wayfarers.

Guthook, a detailed, map-based, satellite app for your phone, claims I only hiked 1.5 miles that day, so that was what I recorded. It was actually 3.5 miles, but who's counting? I was, for sure! It had been my shortest day yet, but also the most relaxing. I was staying at the Plaza motel for forty-four dollars (tax included), and it was perfect. It was clean, the people running it were kind, and I would highly recommend it to all those coming up behind me. Oh, another perk: Linda will do your laundry, which is included in the cost of your night's stay.

I met up with a group of hikers that I had vaguely met over the past miles, Trinity, Hugs, Falls, and Peaches this afternoon. We agreed to meet at a local Mexican restaurant for lunch. The food (and beer) was great, and the company was even better.

Trail angel, Susan (my sister), wanted to know what a typical day's "menu" for a thru-hiker looked like. Well, besides the gourmet/homemade blessings she sent me along the way, an average day's menu:

For breakfast, Pop-Tarts (four hundred calories) and coffee (delicious, but zero calories); for lunch, two flour tortillas (80 calories), plus pepperoni (280 calories) and cheese (an additional 240 calories).

Snacks might include a Cliff bar (260 calories), some dried fruit, and some nuts (170 calories).

Dinner would be Harmony House vegetarian soup mix (three hundred calories) and Ramen noodles (380 calories). All of that comes to a daily total of 2,190 calories—hmmm, no wonder I was losing so much weight.

Thru-hikers typically burn four- to five thousand calories per day. I should rightfully insert that there are some days where those trail angels provide food to supplement and contribute added calories. And, once again, that is so sincerely appreciated. The bag in the picture with the words "Sea To Summit" is my food bag. It currently weighed an estimated twelve pounds, and would take me to Daleville, about a hundred miles from where I was.

Visits into town are for "cameling up." The visits are pre-planned, with a heavy emphasis on giving all-you-can-eat restaurants first and serious consideration. We come, we devour, and we leave before they ever knew what hit them. It's what we do. After all, we are thru-hikers.

DAY 42

I'VE HEARD OF MOTHS EATING A WOOL SWEATER, BUT A FOREST?

21.6 Miles Hiked; 655.2 Miles Total
Start: Plaza Hotel, Pearisburg, Virginia; End: The Captain's Place

Posted Information: Gypsy Moth.

I got up at my usual time that morning and actually had to get my bearings. I was so accustomed to waking up in my tent that I had to reorient myself as to where I was and why I was in a bed. I decided that I "needed" to take one last shower (my third since having checked in the day before). I was glad there wasn't a surcharge for all the hot water I'd used.

I was dressed, packed, and out the door by a quarter past seven. Linda, the manager at the Plaza Motel, saw me leaving and came outside to say goodbye and to wish me good luck. What a sweetheart. I made my way to Hardee's to take advantage of one last serving of their egg-bacon-and-cheese biscuits.

The day before, when I'd slept up at Pearis Ledge, I'd had an incredible view of the town of Pearisburg. I had a funny feeling watching over this distant town far below me. I likened it to the Grinch looking out over Whoville. The view actually got better too, when I woke up in the middle of the night to "answer the call of nature." I crawled out from my tent and was taken by total surprise. The bright town lights below me gave me pause, as it looked like I was looking down at the stars. Stars above me, stars below me—just beautiful.

Sometimes the forest isn't really all that pretty. For example, I walked through a huge area that has been devastated by the gypsy moth. It was incredibly depressing to walk through the carnage. It was difficult to imagine that an insect could do that much damage. As you can read in the picture on the previous page, the US Forest Service had to close a shelter and camping area due to the danger of falling trees—all because of an invasive moth. How this part of the forest could ever recover, I'll never know.

That night, I was camping at the Captain's Place. "Captain" is a gentleman who's property is right on the trail, and he welcomes hikers to camp on his golf-course-level-quality of a yard. It gets better. You have to cross a creek by way of a zip line to get to his property. So very cool! Once you arrive, you are invited to get a soft drink out of the refrigerator on the back porch—and you can have as many as you can drink. There were about twelve of us who camped there that night, and we got to enjoy the warm hospitality of the Captain and the peaceful serenity of the quickly moving creek as it helped provide a restful slumber.

I SAW HER STANDING THERE

The time I saw her standing there—
Oh, how to meet her? How do I dare?
While other fellows thought the same,
I could not falter; I could not wain.
To court this girl, I'd do my best.
I'd act on instinct and beat the rest.
If I failed, would I be less?
It was to be, for she said yes.
And so it goes, this man's happy life
Is owed to this girl, he calls his wife.

(April, 15th, 2017, Day 42, when I couldn't stop thinking about my wife)

DAY 43

I THINK I'D RATHER WALK ON A BED OF RED-HOT COALS

17.3 Miles Hiked; 672.5 Miles Total
Start: The Captain's Place; End: Laurel Creek Shelter

Happy Easter.

Last night, while I had been enjoying my third cold soft drink (thank you, Captain), I saw Acorn hobbling along. "Acorn" was another hiker I'd leapfrogged with these past few weeks. "You okay, Acorn?" I asked. "Yep, it's just that after I take my boots off, I feel like a ninety-year-old man," he replied. Whew, imagine my relief when I discovered I was not the only one. I hate to say, it but misery does love company.

Here's the deal: Your feet are going to outgrow your boots. No kidding, you will gain at least a shoe size from all the hiking. This is due to both the constant pounding and flattening of your feet as well the obvious swelling. I had begun the hike at a size ten, but I was now at least a size eleven—but I was still trying to fit into a size ten boot. It didn't work! I decided I was going to take action. The next town was Daleville, which was another four days' hike. So new boots were going to have to wait until I got there. In the meantime, I had come up with a plan the night before, so I woke up early to implement it.

At a quarter to five that morning, I wrapped all toes with KT Tape (an athletic tape). The rest of my plan was to go commando. No undergarments. That's right, boys and girls, my feet would go naked—no socks. I realized that I had to make more room in my boots, and removing my heavy, wool, hiking socks from the equation just made sense.

Two hours later, at a quarter to seven, I was fed, packed, and pulling myself across the creek via zip line. The yard was full of tents, with many takers of the Captain's generous hospitality. Not a soul was stirring, as I'm certain all were in a comfortable sugar coma from the abundance of free sodas the night before.

Off I went to hike a new day, and guess what? My plan worked! I was like a gazelle, leaping from rock to rock and boulder to boulder. I was like poetry in motion. If I had had tights on, I might have auditioned for the Appalachian Ballet Company. I was unstoppable . . . at least until about lunchtime, that is. Then it was back to walking on shards of glass. I would rather have walked on a bed of red-hot coals. Still, *no pain, no Maine.* I just couldn't get to Daleville fast enough.

The terrain that day was literally a rock-and-boulder scramble; jumping stone to stone and boulder to boulder with several two-thousand-foot ascents. There were no real notable views, just a lot of climbing and walking through more of the gypsy-moth devastation. It had started to rain just as I was coming up to Laurel Creek Shelter at about four thirty that afternoon. My plan had been to hike a few more miles, but the option of staying dry in the shelter won me over. With nobody else there (yet)—fingers crossed it stayed that way—I thought I might sleep in the shelter and avoid having to set up and take down my tent in the rain.

DAY 44

THANK YOU, AUDIE MURPHY

19.2 Miles Hiked; 691.7 Miles Total
Start: Laurel Creek Shelter; End: Stealth Camp

Memorial for Audie Murphy.

Well, I ended up having the shelter to myself. If mice had been cuddling up in my sleeping bag with me, I would have had no idea, as I passed out at eight o'clock to the sounds of a babbling creek. In the morning, I was up early (it's what I do) and hiking by seven. The trail was kind to me, and especially to my feet, with gradual ascents and well-graded trails, for the most part.

I enjoyed my lunch from the top of a rock outcropping, wide open and expansive, overlooking a deep valley with other unnamed mountains as a backdrop. I watched two beautiful brown eagles soar overhead as they looked for their next prey, gliding effortlessly on unseen currents that gave them an unfair advantage over the unsuspecting. I watched, I'll admit, with pleasure and guilt, hoping to witness their success. Perhaps they weren't hunting at all; maybe they were simply watching a thru-hiker eat his lunch on top of a rock outcropping.

It rained most of the day, or a light rain, I should say. I put my rain cover over my pack, but didn't bother with my rain gear. It felt nice, cool; not a drenching rain. I took an afternoon break at Niday Shelter for a snack, and an opportunity to step out of the rain. I took my boots off to allow my feet to dry and reapply some new KT Tape.

Just five miles past Niday Shelter was a memorial for Audie Murphy. The memorial is on a short side trail, and it's not to be missed. Audie Murphy was the most decorated American soldier of World War ll. Apparently, he had died in an airplane crash on that very mountainous site. The memorial was surrounded by stones that had been placed there by visitors, along with other personal effects. Most notable was the large number of military dog tags. It was an honor and quite humbling to spend a few moments there. Thank you, Audie Murphy, for your sacrifice so that I might have the freedoms I enjoy.

My sister had sent me a text message about a week before I got to the memorial, and she was telling me about the moon she was looking at—the same moon I was looking at . . . too easy. After seeing Audie Murphy's memorial, I wondered (if he had been able to), what would his last text to his wife Pat have said?

MURPHY'S STAR

Hello, my love, do truly try
To look toward heaven, up in the sky.
You know I battled and gave a fight
For all that's just, good, and right.
So close to home was not to be;
A tragic flight has taken me.
Do not cry; do not fret.
We'll be together, just not yet.
There is a star by the Milky Way,
Exactly which, I cannot say.
Too many miles stand between;
So many footsteps to be seen.
Yes, I know it's so very far,
But let us find the very same star.
It's up there on this starry night.
If you look, you'll find it right.
If dark clouds do block the light,
Please try again, night after night.
You will fail; don't fret, my dear.
With every step, you'll soon be there.
It's worth it to me; it will do no harm.
Please try each night, till you're in my arms.

(April, 17th, 2017, Day 44)

DAY 45

THE CONTINENTAL DIVIDE

17.9 Miles Hiked; 709.6 Miles Total
Start: Stealth Camp; End: Catawba Shelter

An Unexpected Sign.

With yesterday having been so full, I never mentioned the fact that I'd passed the Continental Divide.

The last place I ever expected to see a sign that indicated I was passing the Continental Divide, was there on the AT. Apparently, the sign marks the location where waters on the west side of Sinking Creek Mountain flow into the Mississippi River and the Gulf of Mexico, and the waters on the east side of the mountain flow into the James River and the Atlantic.

That next day was beautiful, with overcast skies, but no rain, which made for comfortable temperatures. I hiked up to a well-known rock outcropping called the Dragon's Tooth. It was a difficult climb, to say the least, but well worth the side trail. The AT crosses Virginia Route

785 at mile marker 704. I had seen and read about a store that was close by, so I made my way to find it. It was quite close, and another worthy side trip. I had a pint of Moose Tracks ice cream with a Coca-Cola as a chaser. I was now ready to hike some more.

I eventually got to the Catawba Shelter, and so far, I was alone. Did I dare attempt another night in a shelter? I then had a funny thought about two friends and their experiences with the Continental Divide, so I decided to write a poem.

THE STORY OF DRIP AND DROP

Drip and Drop were best of friends;
They vowed this to the very end.
They met that long and rainy day,
And now they're together, all the way.
It's been a long and wild ride;
They even worked at the slip and slide.
Then one day Drip made a claim,
"It looks as though it's gonna rain."
Drop agreed; now they were moving fast.
It looked as though their future was cast.
On their way with the force,
It looked as though they were off course.
"There was a sign! What did it say?"
"I think we may go different ways."
"I do not think we decide.";
"The sign, it said, 'Continental Divide.'"
"Goodbye, my friend, it's time to go.
It's what we do—go with the flow."

(April, 18th, 2017, Day 45)

DAY 46

ON A CLEAR DAY, YOU CAN SEE FOREVER

17.8 Miles Hiked; 727.4 Miles Total
Start: Catawba Shelter; End: Daleville, Virginia

Whistler Contemplates Fog.

Drip and Drop decided to make an all-day appearance. I'd been lucky enough to be the only occupant at Catawba Shelter the previous night. The plus to that was not having to set up and take down my tent. This was welcomed, as it rained all night. It was also quite cold. I wanted to get an early start in the morning because I had planned a full schedule. I was up at five thirty, dressed in full rain gear and hiking by seven o'clock. First on my to-do list was to hike up to McAfee Knob. This outcropping is said to be the most photographed location on the AT.

When I arrived, I was the only one there (no one to take my picture), and it was too foggy anyway. I hiked on to hit the next location on my to-do list. Tinker Cliffs was just another 4.5 miles away. The

Tinker Cliffs are known for the quarter mile of cliffs with a westerly view. I bet the views are great when it's not *foggy*. Does fog actually serve a practical purpose? Thanks a lot, Drip and Drop!

I stopped in at Lambert's Meadow Shelter for a quick and early lunch, and a chance to dry off.

The next item on my master plan was to get into Daleville. I got into town right at two thirty that afternoon, checked into the Super 8 Motel, showered, and did laundry. The Three Li'l Pigs Barbecue for dinner was definitely happening. I'd made a decision while hiking there that I was also going to take a zero tomorrow. I needed to resupply and get new boots, and honestly, I needed to give myself a day of rest—especially my feet.

DAY 47

SO I HAVE TO TELL THE TRUTH

0 Miles Hiked; 727.4 Miles Total
Start: Daleville, Virginia; End: Daleville, Virginia

Not a Momma Bear and Cub, after All.

You know, I just have to tell the truth. A couple of days prior, I'd come upon what I thought was my first bear encounter. I was cranking along at a brisk pace, when I was caught off guard and my heart skipped a beat—or two, or maybe even three. Well, as you can see from the photo, it was just a momma cow and her calf. I thought about hamburgers the rest of the day.

It's true, it's true, Three Li'l Pigs has great barbecue, and I highly recommend it. As an added bonus, thru-hikers receive a free (huge) banana pudding for dessert.

Even though I was taking a zero that day, I still started my day early. I made it down to the Super 8 breakfast room at six thirty and filled up on the early-morning offerings. After breakfast, I was off to the local Kroger for my resupply. I also made a trip to the local outfitters. Unfortunately, I couldn't find boots that felt right, so I decided to try a thin pair of hiking socks instead. I figured that I had been hiking the past three days without socks and my feet had felt much better. My boots still had a couple of hundred miles to offer up as well, so I thought I'd give it a shot. I walked all day around town and they felt pretty darn good. I guess they would get the "trail trial" tomorrow.

I also purchased a quilt and sleeping-bag liner, and sent my three-season bag home. I know, I know, it was a bit early to be dumping the warmth of my three-season bag, but it weighed too much, and was way too bulky. It weighed three pounds, seven ounces. My new quilt weighted only one pound, and the liner was nine ounces—nearly two pounds less, and far less volume taken up in my pack (more room for food?). I still had my base layer that I could wear on those certain colder nights that could still occur.

I ran into Fish, Radio, and Sherlock that day. Fish was meeting a friend he had worked with in the past and Radio was running his errands in town, so Sherlock and I had dinner and a beer at Three Li'l Pigs (and another free banana pudding). I was planning on an early start the next morning so I would hit the breakfast downstairs at six and be pounding the trail by seven.

Knowing that I had to mail my sleeping bag, I asked the Super 8 desk clerk where the post office was in town. She gave me directions, which placed it about a mile away. There I was, having hiked over seven hundred miles, and now that I was in town, a one-mile walk seemed to be a great distance. It's funny how one's perspective can change in less than twenty-four hours.

DAY 48

ALONG CAME A SPIDER

25 Miles Hiked; 752.4 Miles Total
Start: Daleville, Virginia; End: Cove Mountain Shelter

Cars Speeding by on the Blue Ridge Parkway.

Could the forest really have changed that much in just one day?

I was up at five thirty, boots on the trail an hour later, and two things really stood out to me as soon as I found myself in the woods that morning. First, as if out of nowhere, and just since I'd been off the trail for a day, the trees had leafed out. I love that pale-green new leaf growth. It feels so fresh, new, and alive. Spring was springing, and I got to have a front-row seat. Sure, I'd seen Spring come before, but now I had the opportunity to observe it in all its glory. Free from outside interferences, free from worldly interruptions and outside (or would it be "inside"?) influences.

The second thing I noticed right away was all the spider webs crossing the trail. The first hiker on the trail in the morning gets to bust through the webs spun by the spiders overnight. It became obvious that I was that first hiker on the trail as it was so annoying to constantly have them in my face. What a waste of time for those spiders. What exactly is it they're trying to catch, anyway?

The trail was kind to me that day, with gradual ascents and descents and virtually no rocks, which made for quick and easier miles. That section of Virginia follows the Blue Ridge Parkway for about a hundred miles. It crisscrosses the Parkway numerous times, and is so close, you can count the passing cars. The whole time, unbeknownst to those drivers, there are hikers on the unseen AT. I had driven the Blue Ridge Parkway many times over the years, and had no idea the AT was literally mere feet from the road.

So about those spiders . . .

WEBSTER THE SPIDER

Webster the spider went to work each day
To catch a hiker, is what they say.
He'd work all day; he'd work all night.
He'd spin his web good and tight.
To catch a hiker, difficult as it seems,
It had always been his lifelong dream.
Early one morning, when his spinning was done,
He prayed for a hiker—Oh, Lord! Just one!
Along came a hiker, taking great big strides.
Webster knew he had to run and hide.
The hiker was stuck now, and could no longer walk,
When along came Webster to have a talk.
"I've done it! I've done it! I caught you! You're mine!"
The hiker looked at him and said, "There's no time."
"Ridiculous hiker, I'll serve you with grog."
"Not today, spider! Look out for that FROG!

(April, 21st, 2017, Day 48)

Day 49

A Very Wet and Crazy Day

17.2 Miles Hiked; 769.6 Miles Total
Start: Cove Mountain Shelter; End: Thunder Hill Shelter

Mr. Rock, Please Wait to Fall.

It rained all night and again all day. The weather report was calling for more of the same the next two days, as well. I caught a bit of good luck that morning, as there was a thirty-minute break in the rain just as I was breaking camp. It's kind of funny how, no matter what you do, you're going to get soaked; rain just has its way with you. It's going to find what's dry and make it wet—no matter what. At one point I found myself standing under a huge tree, and thought that I was hardly getting wet. About 2.5 seconds later, I realized that I wasn't getting any closer to Maine, either—so I hiked on.

 I finally had to quit hiking at four o'clock that afternoon. I was tired, cold, and soaked to the bone. The first step once I made it to Thunder Hill Shelter was to get out of my wet clothes. The second step was to get hot food in my stomach. Besides the heavy rainfall, there had been some tough climbs. I was not looking forward to tomorrow, as it was supposed to be even worse. Okay, on three, everyone! One, two, three . . . no rain, no Maine!

The trail-trial with my new socks had gone well that day, and I'd achieved another milestone: I was now one-third of the way through my journey.

Day 50

WHAT A WAY TO END THE DAY

25.1 Miles Hiked; 794.7 Miles Total
Start: Thunder Hill Shelter; End: Punchbowl Shelter

Memorial for Ottie Cline Powell.

I woke up early (at four thirty) that morning, I suppose because I was in my sleeping bag by six thirty the night before. I thought about going back to sleep, but realized that it had stopped raining. I dread taking my tent down while it's raining, so that was motivation enough. It was a pretty cold morning, as well. Getting dressed was not something I was looking forward to because my clothes were still soaked and cold from the rain yesterday. At one point, I had seriously thought about wearing my dry camp clothes, but knew I'd regret it later if I did. So I bit the bullet, and changed into those stinky, wet, and cold clothes.

I had boots on the trail that morning at a quarter past six, and no idea how many miles I would do that day. The weather would help make that decision. As it turned out, the rain was light, which made for cool and productive hiking. In fact, it turned out to be my highest mileage day to date.

After crossing the James River Foot Bridge (named after William T. Foot), I met Ant Man and his friend Mike. Ant Man was just getting back on the trail after a couple days off while visiting his friend Mike. "Ant Man" got out of Mike's van and Mike drove off but they both let me know to be on the lookout for trail magic. A short time later, I found Mike further up the trail at a creek crossing laying out some soft drinks and beer.

Toward the very end of a long day of hiking, I came across another memorial, which was for a very young child. This was a tough one to see. On November 9th, 1891, four year old Ottie Cline Powel left school during a snow storm and got lost. He was found five months later on the very spot of this memorial. Watch out for those babies and may God bless every one of them.

DAY 51

NOT A TALE; I'M DONE—FOR THE DAY, THAT IS

9.5 Miles Hiked; 804.2 Miles Total
Start: Punchbowl Shelter; End: Brown Mountain Creek Shelter

Crossing the James River.

It had rained like crazy all night and into the morning. At around six that morning, it sounded as though it was slowing down. I jumped into action and packed as quickly as I could. I got back on the trail by seven, with big plans that just never developed.

At one point, I came to a creek that had swollen from the rain so much that I actually paced the shore like an ape looking for a safe way across. I finally realized that I would have to ford the torrential force of this usually calm creek. I had thought about taking my boots off, but why bother? At this point everything was already soaked.

When I finally got to Brown Mountain Creek Shelter, Will-Da-Beast was there. I had not seen "Will-Da-Beast" since the time that I was certain that all the hikers had been captured by that witch with the gingerbread house. I asked him when he had arrived, and he laughed. "Are you kidding me?" he replied. "I got here last night, and decided I wasn't hiking in that mess." I guess that's when I decided I needed to have enough sense to get out of the rain. Hey, I had plenty of food, and there was no shortage of water either.

The day's milestone? I had now passed the eight-hundred-mile mark!

So, as is my tendency to do, I couldn't stop thinking of Little Ottie Cline Powell and the memorial I'd passed yesterday. What was that little boy thinking? What was he looking for? How long did they search for him? How difficult it must have been to find his body five months after he'd gotten lost.

I was done! It was exactly one o'clock in the afternoon, and I was in my tent, sleeping quilt, and dry clothes. I just couldn't take anymore of the rain. I was at Brown Mountain Creek Shelter, where I stopped for lunch and was shivering so hard that I thought my teeth would shatter. The rain let up just as I was thinking about what I should do. I made the decision to set up my tent and climb in. I had to get out of those wet clothes.

LITTLE OTTIE

Oh, little Ottie, not yet five,
So full of dreams and so alive.
You ventured off from school, they say.
To run? To hide? To skip or play?
Was it in you to explore?
The warmth and safety you ignored.
They searched the very mountainside
That you had chosen to abide.
And when all was given and all lost hope,
How did your mother begin to cope?
A stone now marks where you were found.
I pray for you while I'm homeward bound.

(April, 24th, 2017, Day 51)

Day 52

YOU GOTTA KNOW WHEN TO TAKE A BREAK

8.1 Miles Hiked; 812.3 Miles Total
Start: Brown Mountain Creek Shelter; End: Budget Inn, Buena Vista,
Virginia

View from Four Thousand Feet.

After much rest, I awoke at four that morning with a get-up-and-go attitude. It was still raining, of course, but I felt I had to get moving. I ate, changed (back into my wet clothes), packed my backpack, and waited patiently in my tent for a break in the rain. When that never occurred, I just crawled out and took the tent down in the pouring rain. The issue with rain isn't hiking in it; that's no big deal. The problem is when you have toenails coming off and blisters that need to dry out to heal, but are swimming in your boots instead.

Walking had become painful—and you need to be able to walk when you're hiking. I had just made it to the top of Cole Mountain when I ran into two students from Southern Virginia University, Kevin and Lauren, who were out for a hike. I joked with them about being out there in the nasty weather. They told me that they were supposed to be studying for finals, but hiking in the rain had won out. I hobbled down to Hog Camp Gap, and saw what I thought must have been their car. I thought to myself that if they came walking back down the trail, I'd come right out and ask for a ride to a motel. Don't you know that I no sooner turned around, and there they were. Kevin and Lauren didn't hesitate to give me a ride. Many thanks to these two special trail angels who I believe were sent to assist me in my time of need.

I was now at the Budget Inn (that's another story) in Buena Vista, Virginia for the night, and to be honest, I thought it would possibly be two nights. I cut some skin from around one toe, applied mupirocin ointment for infection (that was rearing it's ugly head), and pulled one of those toenails off that had just been hanging on.

I used the blow dryer in my room to dry out my boots, but I first had to wring out the insoles by hand because of how soaked they were. I had already cleaned and dried all my equipment and clothes. I was ready to hike, but I needed my feet to be just as ready.

The motel was booked solid with hikers who had all had enough sense to get out of the rain. I'm just a bit stubborn, and tend to take a bit longer to come to the proper conclusion.

When I stopped at Rockfish Gap on Thursday to pick up a re-supply box that Lauren, trail angel, had shipped there for me, I had originally been planning on taking a short day, and possibly a zero. Instead, I decided I would just swing by once I left the motel, pick up my package, and hike on. The best laid plans . . .

DAY 53

NEW WHEELS, TRAIL-READY

0 Miles Hiked; 812.3 Miles Total
Start: Budget Inn, Buena Vista, Virginia; End: Budget Inn, Buena Vista,
Virginia

New Wheels.

It was a day for taking control and serious action. After breakfast, I found the local pharmacy and put together a foot repair kit: small scissors for cutting and removing dead skin around blisters, bandages, Band-Aids, and first aid tape. Up next was a trip to Lexington, Virginia, which is a great historic town, and has a fantastic outfitters. The Maury Express, a three-county public transit system, took me there for the rate of fifty cents. It runs every hour on a continuous loop until six in the evening.

Walkabout Outfitters in Lexington is a full-service outfitters that has an enormous inventory to meet your every need. I decided to go with an Oboz trail-running shoe instead of a boot; they were lighter, not waterproof (which meant they would dry faster when they got wet), and had a bigger toe box. My boots were a size ten; these were a size eleven and a half. This really didn't mean a whole lot, as different manufacturers produce according to their own size specifications. It's pretty common, when long-distance hiking, to have to later size up or change styles, i.e., go from boots to trail runners. In fact, I'd spoken to one hiker a couple weeks ago who was already on her fourth pair. She just couldn't find what worked for her.

The next task at hand was to get a ride back to Hog Camp Gap to take up where I'd left off the day before. Aubrey Taylor was a local gentleman who offered shuttle rides. He would be picking me up at seven o'clock the next morning, which meant I should be back on the trail by eight.

Ironically, it's been so typical and predictable that the only days I've taken off the trail have been beautiful, weather-wise. Today was no exception. I almost felt—no, not almost, I did feel—guilty for not having laid down some miles. In the end, I knew I made the right decision to get off the trail and take care of myself (my feet). After all, Katahdin would still be there.

Lexington is one of those small towns that you will want to visit. It is a quaint and extremely historic town that warrants spending time to explore—time that I unfortunately did not have. Instead, it was added to the quickly expanding list of spots I now considered to have "must-return" status.

Lexington, Virginia was named in 1778. It was one of the first of what would be many American places named after Lexington, Massachusetts, which is known for being the place where the first shot was fired in the American Revolution.

Union General David Hunter led a raid on Virginia Military Institute during the American Civil War. Robert E. Lee and Stonewall Jackson are buried in Lexington. It is the site of the only house Jackson ever owned, now open to the public as a museum. Cyrus McCormick invented the horse-drawn mechanical reaper at his family's farm in Rockbridge County, and a statue of McCormick is located on the Washington and Lee University campus. McCormick Farm is now owned by Virginia Tech, and is a satellite agricultural research center.

DAY 54

MAKING TRACKS AGAIN

21.7 Miles Hiked; 834 Miles Total
Start: Budget Inn, Buena Vista, Virginia; End: Harpers Creek Shelter

Aubrey "Piney" Taylor and Whistler.

Boy, it was good to be back on the trail again. As usual, I was up early, dressed, and at Hardee's by six for two biscuits with steak and their bottomless cup of coffee. I made it back to the motel by a quarter to seven, and Aubrey "Piney" Taylor was already there. I grabbed my pack and trekking poles, and jumped into the passenger seat of his 1990 F150 truck. Piney ended up being exactly what I had imagined from speaking to him over the phone. He is the nicest guy you could ever imagine. In fact, he reminded me of my buddy and neighbor, Eric. Piney is 76 years old, and has no interest in not going to work every day—sounds like Eric already—just a salt-of-the-earth kind of guy that really enjoys helping out thru-hikers. In fact, his business card says "helping hikers since 1959" (the year I was born). He is a great story teller, as well, and kept me entertained for the entire ride back to Hog Camp Gap.

Hikers: Call Piney Taylor at (540) 261-6998 or (540) 460-3527 if you need a shuttle at a fair price. Piney covers a long section of the trail, including Punchbowl Mountain and Salt Log Gap, and will go beyond if needed. Call him early—he stays real busy.

It was a really good day in terms of the weather (although it was now pouring as I sat inside my tent). It had been sunny, with cool breezes, and ended up being a kind trail for a hiker who'd been off trail for a day and a half. The new shoes seemed to be working for me, as well. I took a couple short breaks during my hike, changed the dressing on a couple of toes and changed into new socks, as well. It looked like everything was healing as I'd hoped.

FEET

Oh, my aching feet.
Step up, step down, and repeat.
The boots, they hug the feet too tight.
Perhaps the size is not quite right.
They pinch and rub and really squeeze.
Perhaps it's time for new ones, please.
If you need a warning, Whistler,
I'll oblige you with a blister.
If you take good care of me,
Katahdin, you will surely see.

(April, 27th, 2017, Day 54)

DAY 55

VIRGINIA BLUES? MAYBE

22 Miles Hiked; 856 Miles Total
Start: Harpers Creek Shelter; End: Paul C. Wolfe Shelter

Rocks on Top of Rocks.

There are 544 miles of the AT running through Virginia, which accounts for nearly one quarter of the trail. They say that thru-hikers get tired of hiking the same state and there is a feeling of a lack of progress. That feeling has been dubbed, "The Virginia Blues." I had not felt that way until perhaps now. Of the twenty-two miles I'd hiked this day, I would have to say eighteen of those were rock scrambles. It was very difficult, with a couple of big climbs and extremely rocky—and that would be an understatement. Three Ridges Mountain is a four-thousand-foot summit with steep climbs over three miles, and that started as soon as I left Harpers Creek that morning. It was difficult for me to find my hiking "groove" or the right hiking gear. I'd started at seven that morning, and didn't finish those twenty-two miles until six thirty that evening—a real slow one for me.

When I had finally arrived at Paul C. Wolfe Shelter, Fresh, Karaoke, and Maps (three guys I had met over the miles and who had passed me earlier that day due to my slower pace that day) were already there. After enjoying our dinner together that evening, I asked them if they wouldn't mind telling me why they were hiking the AT. I let them know that I wanted to know what motivated other thru-hikers, and that I would be writing their responses in my journal later.

Maps was first up; a young guy, probably twenty-four years old. He had always enjoyed walking, and wanted to experience the various landscapes while physically challenging himself.

Fresh was thirty years old, and hoped to be to Katahdin by mid-July for his birthday. He had a well-paying job as a business analyst, but sat in a cubicle every day and wanted more in his life. He'd read a lot of adventure books, and hiking the AT had always been a dream of his. Finally, he, too, wanted to challenge himself.

Karaoke was a young man from Germany, and was just out of high school. He would be starting sports management school in the fall, so he'd had time to hike the AT. He'd first learned about it when he'd seen a documentary at age twelve, and as a result, had always wanted to thru-hike. He, too, said he wanted to challenge himself.

My personal observation of the thru-hikers I've met, and have spent any amount of time with, is that they tend to be highly motivated. They get up early, hike their miles, and go to bed early, just to repeat the process the next day, and each day thereafter. We hike like we mean it.

And now I came to the realization that to continue my hike I was going to have to take some time off to allow my body to heal. So, I let my family and those who had been following me know that I was going to take a week off the trail. I was going to take this week to visit my sister and brother-in-law in Mississippi. They had just moved into their new home, which I had not seen yet and thought that now was the right time. I could have gone home to Nova Scotia, but to be honest, I did not want to go home. Home was where I was supposed to walk to. If I went there now would I have gotten back on the trail? A week off the trail would hopefully allow my feet and other physical ailments time to heal. Hiking twenty-plus miles each day would never allow me to fully recover. I hated it, but knew I needed this. The prize waiting in Maine was just too important to me.

DAY 56

THAT WAS EASY

5 Miles Hiked; 861 Miles Total
Start: Paul C. Wolfe Shelter; End: Rockfish Gap

Steak Dinner.

I'd thought I was going to sleep like a stone the night before, but not so. I guess I'd just had too much on my mind. I woke up at three thirty that morning and checked on flights to Mobile, Alabama—wow, it was more than $600 for a one-way ticket. Instead, I looked up car rental locations in Waynesboro, Virginia, and found that Enterprise had a local office. My car was now booked for the week.

I hiked the last five miles to Rockfish Gap, and another half mile to the Colony Motel for the resupply box my daughter-in-law had shipped there. Once the Enterprise office had opened at nine o'clock, I phoned them, and they came to pick me up—that had been easy! The drive to my sister and brother-in-law's house was supposed to be right at thirteen hours, but I made good time (wink, wink) and made it in twelve, including stops.

Driving a car felt strange at first. After nearly two months of walking wherever I'd needed to go, driving seemed so . . . so fast. It also afforded an interesting review of the weeks upon weeks of hiking I'd done. As I drove south on the highway, I would see signs for all the locations and places I had recently been. It was as though my life was in rewind.

Once I got to my sister and brother-in-law's new home, I was handed a beer. I got the nickel tour of their new home, and sat down to the biggest bone-in ribeye steak I had ever seen. It was literally hanging off the plate, served with mushrooms and asparagus in a lemon sauce (I'd been craving a real vegetable). Dessert was five of Susan's blueberry muffins I'd seen on a plate in the kitchen (I think they were supposed to be for breakfast).

I believe it was close to two in the morning when Susan walked me to the guest house. Of course, my sister had that refrigerator stocked for my stay (I would be checking out those interesting beers tomorrow). In the meantime, I was going to pass out.

Day 57

EAT, REST, EAT, REST, EAT, REST

0 Miles Hiked; 861 Miles Total
Start: Off Trail; End: Off Trail

Guest House: My Home for the Week.

I didn't get up until eight the next morning, after having gone to bed so late. Susan and I had coffee together and planned out our day. I had seen their new home when I'd arrived, but not the property. Sitting on thirty-plus acres, the house and guest house face each another, with about 150 yards between them. This area is cleared with beautiful oak, pine, and magnolia trees, and some specimen trees scattered throughout. There are several, large, fenced paddocks for livestock, and stables and additional outbuildings, while the remainder of the property is fully wooded.

My plan for the day was mostly eat, relax, and repeat those things throughout the day. My brother-in-law, Top, had a sixteen-year-old young man coming to the house to work the property all day. Top has always worked well with young men, and is a strong mentor when he's teaching them life skills. I think that comes from his time in the marines, when he and his fellow marines had to watch over each other for their very survival.

Susan baked bread, and I later hung all her pictures she'd been wanting to get up on the walls of their beautiful country home.

When dinner time arrived, I learned that we would have to have ribeye steaks again, because the freezer door had been left open and the steaks had thawed out. Needless to say, it was my pleasure to assist with that problem.

DAY 58

AQUA BLAZING

0 Miles Hiked; 861 Miles Total
Start: Off Trail; End: Off Trail

Ruins Going into Waynesboro, Virginia.

It was day fifty-eight of my thru-hike, and on that day of my great adventure, I went shopping with my sister for granite countertops and major appliances. Susan had had enough of the 1980s appliances in her new home, so she took me with her to research the new ones she would be ordering. Hey, what else was I going to do? Besides, I had the opportunity to spend time with my sister, and the best part was that we ate shrimp po'boys at a roadside food truck. Well, maybe the best part was spending quality time with my sister.

Tomorrow was looking like a kayak paddle day. Susan is a paddling freak, and has a collection of some of the top kayaks produced. She is an avid paddler, and competes in some of the major races throughout North America. In fact, I would be her ground support in next year's Missouri 340, which is a three hundred and forty mile race on the Missouri River. I, myself, am a kayaking novice, which means I greatly respect her for her abilities in the sport.

I'd seen a huge improvement, starting the day before, on my feet and shin splints. I also visited an outfitters for a different pair of trail-running shoes, as the other pair I'd purchased just hadn't felt right. My new shoes were the Altra Lone Peak 3.0, which have a great reputation on the trail. These had a wider toe box and a flat, zero-drop heel, which make for a more comfortable and almost barefoot, natural feel. As you may recall, the other shoes (that I'd only hiked in for two days) were made by Oboz. They, too, have a great reputation, but they have a rolled sole which wraps up the side of the shoe that had me constantly rolling my ankles. (Had I just avoided a possible future injury?)

DAY 59

PLAY DAY

0 Miles Hiked; 861 Miles Total
Start: Off Trail; End: Off Trail

Whistler and Sister Susan on the Water.

Susan came over to the guest house that morning with coffee for the two of us. We sat and planned our day of kayaking. We needed to move the carrier from her Jeep to Top's vehicle first, and then load the two boats we would be paddling. Once we'd gathered the paddles, PFDs, safety equipment, and snacks, we were on our way. The weather was absolutely perfect for a leisurely paddle, barely a ripple on the water and there was virtually no other activity, like speeding motor boats. Susan took the opportunity to do some sprints, part of her training regimen. I, on the other hand, took it easy and just enjoyed the peacefulness the water had to offer. (I was not training for a race.) We paddled the length of the lake, and after about four hours, loaded the boats and headed back to the house.

Tomorrow was a work day for us. Susan was going to work in her vegetable garden, Top was always working on something, and I was going to do some minor carpentry work on Susan's closets.

My feet and shins had continued to feel much better. I was excited about getting back to good health, and was really looking forward to getting back on the trail.

DAY 60

PLAY DAY

0 Miles Hiked; 861 Miles Total
Start: Off Trail; End: Off Trail

Susan's Bread.

I was really enjoying my early-morning coffee time with Susan. It gave us the opportunity to just chat, catch up on our lives, and to plan for the day.

This day's plan was to get some actual work done—no more playing around. I was in my element, taking on some carpentry work in Susan's closet. Susan worked in her garden, and Top went nonstop on everything. It did start to rain in the late afternoon, so Susan baked bread and I finished hanging up their pictures/art.

The rain never stopped, and turned into a huge thunderstorm. Boy, I was sure glad I wasn't hiking in that.

Susan was putting on a lunch the next day for an old friend who was coming to visit them, and later, the plan for the evening was to attend a minor league baseball game.

DAY 61

HITTING THE WALL

0 Miles Hiked; 861 Miles Total
Start: Off Trail; End: Off Trail

Whistler, Susan and Top at the Ballpark.

This was probably the first day in sixty days where I actually relaxed. Sure, I'd had a week off the trail now, but it had been a busy week. In fact, I'd finally hit the wall after staying up way too late, really enjoying my time with Susan and Top; most nights I'd gotten only five or six hours of sleep after playing, eating, drinking, and working all day.

I woke up late and took an afternoon nap, which is not something I ever do. I skipped Susan's luncheon that she had put together for their friend Betty, at Susan's insistence. No argument from me; the sleep was amazing. We did go to the ball game, and sat in the Mercedes Benz skybox, which included great food and made for a relaxing night. We were home and I was in bed before ten o'clock. Tomorrow was going to be another "work day." I was going to hook up Susan's stereo, install Top's air conditioner in his shop, and bring the Christmas decorations up to the attic.

I was so pleased with how my shin splints had healed, and my feet now felt fantastic. I was so ready to start back on the trail. Sure, I felt bad that I'd lost that time on the trail, but I was so pleased to have had the time with family—a pretty good trade-off!

DAY 62

IT'S LIKE A THREE-RING CIRCUS

0 Miles Hiked; 861 Miles Total
Start: Off Trail; End: Off Trail

Top the Clown and Two of His Circus Performers.

Susan, Top, and I started the day with a huge breakfast, and then we hit the ground running. Yes, we'd played hard that week, but today was a work-hard day. I love it when you can put a check mark next to those items on the to-do list. How many times have we all said, "If I had another set of hands, I'd be able to complete . . . "? Dinner was a quick and easy meal of leftovers in front of the TV while the movie *Hacksaw Ridge* was on, and bed was going to come early. Tomorrow was my last day with my dear sister and brother-in-law. There were a couple of smaller tasks to complete, but it was now time for me to pack up my pack and prepare for my thirteen-hour drive back to Waynesboro, Virginia. I had miles to make up—and I had the good health that would allow me to do so.

DAY 63

ALL GOOD THINGS MUST COME TO AN END

0 Miles Hiked; 861 Miles Total
Start: Off Trail; End: Off Trail

Leaving Susan and Top's Home.

I returned to the guest house after a full day spent with Susan and Top. It had been a full day, yes, but it was also very relaxing before heading back to Virginia to continue my thru-hike. I hadn't wanted to add a week to my hike, but I knew I'd done the right thing in taking it off. I'm not sure I could ever express my appreciation to Susan and Top for all they did for me. Susan took it as a personal challenge to put some meat on my bones—for which she can claim success (I'd gained two pounds after that week). My feet and shin splints had healed, and I was anxious to regain my trail legs.

Susan and I had an early-morning coffee date, and then I would be on the road by seven. It wouldn't be long before I was going to be writing my daily journal post from the trail again.

DAY 64

BACK TO THE FUTURE

0 Miles Hiked; 861 Miles Total
Start: Off Trail; End: Off Trail

Back to Trail Food; Hydrating Tomorrow's Dinner.

I was up at five thirty that morning, dressed and finished packing by six. I'd had a couple bowls of cereal when Susan came in with coffee and two bacon-egg-and-cheese sliders—my second breakfast. We chatted until seven, which was my agreed-upon departure time. It was tough for both of us to say goodbye. The time there was such a terrific respite for me. Yes, I was a week behind now, but the time I'd been able to spend with my sister was invaluable to me.

I was also *so* ready to be back on the trail. Thank you, Lord, for a nearly 1,800-mile round-trip that had delivered me safely to my destinations.

It was nine thirty at night, and I'd just arrived back to Waynesboro, Virginia. My first stop was at a gas station to top off the rental car tank. There was a sign advertising a special where if you bought two twenty-ounce Cokes for two bucks, you got two free hot dogs—dinner was taken care of! While there, I also started preparing for the next night's dinner, and got some hot water to rehydrate my Harmony House dinner.

I was just going to pull into the Enterprise parking lot and sleep in the car, where it would be warm, as it was supposed to get down to twenty-nine degrees that night. They opened at eight and they would give me a ride to the trailhead. The weather was looking like there would be clear skies and a high of sixty-five, as well. I love it when a plan comes together.

TIME

Seconds and minutes measured;
Our time, sacred and treasured.
It's importance in chronology,
Misspent with no apology.
Coveted not to waste;
Lost with our failed pace.
Unable to regain,
What is left, is what remains.
My wish to give what is mine
To those I love: the gift of time.

(May, 7th, 2017, Day 64)

DAY 65

I'M BACK!

20.8 Miles Hiked; 881.8 Miles Total
Start: Rockfish Gap; End: Blackrock Hut

Whistler with His Shenandoah National Park Permit.

What a difference a week makes. I'd thought sleeping in my rental car was a good idea, but it was awful. I pulled into the Enterprise parking lot and picked a secluded parking spot. I pulled my sleeping quilt out of my pack, climbed into the back seat, and found it impossible to get comfortable. I finally fell asleep after one in the morning, but woke up at three thirty and couldn't get back to sleep. The manager at Enterprise checked in my rental before they were even open, and had one of his associates drive me to the trailhead.

I had my Shenandoah National Park permit filed, and was hiking by eight that morning. Unlike the Great Smoky Mountains National Park, Shenandoah National Park does not charge a fee for your permit, but they will fine you if you don't have one. While filling out my permit, I heard someone call out my name. I turned around and found that Floater was standing behind me. I was really surprised to see her after my extended leave, as I thought I wouldn't be seeing anyone I knew again. It turns out that she and Onion had been off the trail because Onion had sustained an ankle injury. She was a strong hiker, but unfortunately Onion was now off the trail for good.

I was so appreciative of the easy conditions the trail offered up that day, because I hiked all day like a zombie. I kept tripping over my own feet, and actually half considered laying down on the trail for a nap. I will tell you that eight days off the trail made for some "soft" legs, but the biggest difference I noticed was in my lung capacity. Nevertheless, twenty miles was still good for my first day back, and I really didn't want to overdo it anyway.

As I hiked along that day, I found that I was getting into my hiking groove. It's difficult to describe, but it was almost like a trance. I was cooking along at a great pace, making great time, when I suddenly found myself crossing a dirt road. Out of the corner of my eye, I spied a guy sitting on a stone wall, eating a bag of chocolate doughnuts. I gave a quick wave, said hello, asked if he was doing all right, and continued on.

As I was coming off the dirt road and reentering the woods, I told myself to turn back around and introduce myself to the guy. I guess I took him by surprise, or he might have been suspicious. Like, "Hey, what do you want? No, you can't have any of my chocolate doughnuts." Anyway, his name was Scooby, and after we went through the formal introductions, we then hiked pretty much all day together.

Scooby had started on March 13, eight days after my own start date, and was making really good time. I wasn't sure I would be able to continue at his same pace, as he was six feet six and had a seriously long stride. We would see how tomorrow went. Unfortunately, I was still having an issue with shin splints in my right leg.

In the time that I'd been gone from the trail for over a week, I noticed how lush the forest had become now. It had really filled in. Also, there were butterflies everywhere. You simply couldn't believe how many of those "flying flowers" there were; just so beautiful. We had also traded the Blue Ridge Parkway for the Skyline Drive. In fact, the trail follows Skyline Drive so closely that I ended up crossing it nine times that day. Tonight's temperatures were going to be close to freezing. Of course, I had already sent all my winter gear home. I guessed I would have to just snuggle up to a bear. Tomorrow's hiking conditions looked like they were going to be somewhat similar (based on my guide book).

DAY 66

ANOTHER BEAUTIFUL DAY IN PARADISE

21.5 Miles Hiked; 903.3 Miles Total
Start: Blackrock Hut; End: Hightop Hut

Whistler, Ready for Take Off.

What a difference a great night of sleep can make. Sure, it had been darn cold, but with three shirts, two pairs of shorts, socks, and gloves, I was warm in my sleeping bag liner and quilt. I was up early for oatmeal and coffee, and was packed and hiking by seven. I felt great, and the trail was kind to me once again. I love the Shenandoahs.

I hiked pretty much all day with Scooby, Floater, and Hodgepodge. You tend to hike apart and meet up again throughout the day, as everyone goes at their own pace. We met for lunch at Loft Mountain Campground, where I think we all ate too much. Couldn't help it; the food was too plentiful and so good.

While hiking early that morning, I met Chip and Emily, who were hiking together. They were a father-daughter duo who were section hiking for a week, which was something they did together every year. What great memories they were making together.

There were a couple of differences between what I saw on the trail previously compared to what I'd seen in Shenandoah National Park. One was the unique wayfinding posts. All wayfinding signs up to that point had been made of wood, which, to be honest, does show its wear over time. The signs here were concrete posts, with steel bands and an embossed directory on each one. The other difference was that at Shenandoah National Park, the shelters were called "huts." The park was neat, clean, and well organized. The Loft Mountain Campground was impeccable, while the camp store there was run like a well oiled machine. Bathrooms and showers looked like they belonged in a fine resort. A real class act, and proof that this government agency was making good use of tax payers' dollars.

Today's milestone: I'd now hiked over nine hundred miles.

DAY 67

LIFE IS GOOD IN THE SHENANDOAHS

23.8 Miles Hiked; 927.1 Miles Total
Start: Hightop Hut; End: Rock Spring Hut

Deer within Twenty Feet of Camp.

I was in my tent and sound asleep by eight o'clock last night, as I was just plain worn out after being up at five and on the trail by a quarter to seven.

Today's hike ended up having a few pretty good climbs, but overall the trail was kind. I hiked pretty much all day with Scooby, and we both took full advantage of all the park had to offer. The park has a number of campgrounds throughout, and the trail skirts right along them. That, of course, meant *food*. One of our stops was at Lewis Mountain Campground and Cabins. I had a cold beer to wash down my corn chips. Scooby had ice cream and a box of cookies. Our next stop was going to be eight miles up the trail: Big Meadows Lodge.

Big Meadows Lodge has what they call a "wayside." Waysides are restaurants that are for tourists, and work out pretty well for thru-hikers, too. The lodge is also known for their blackberry milkshakes. It's a thru-hiker tradition to partake of one of these milkshakes. I had mine with an order of fries. I thought I was actually gaining weight!

While we were having our dinner at camp that night, Scooby and I discovered that another wayside required just a four-mile hike in the morning, and they opened at eight. We would be leaving at six thirty the next morning, and would hopefully be there when they unlocked the doors. I saw a big breakfast in my future; no Pop-Tarts tomorrow.

Unfortunately, the weather forecast called for rain the next several days. If ever a meteorologist was to be wrong, I thought, please let that be now. We had been so blessed with perfect weather that week, but all good things—good weather—must come to an end (darn it!).

DAY 68

RAIN, RAIN, GO AWAY

22.5 Miles Hiked; 949.6 Miles Total
Start: Rock Spring Hut; End: Stealth Camp, Elkwallow Wayside

Princess Poppy Enjoying Breakfast.

What a thunderstorm we'd had last night. It rained and thundered so violently, it shook the mountain I was camping on. Funny thing, though, Scooby never heard any of it. The storm broke right at six the next morning, and the radar showed that we would have a break for a couple of hours before the next band rolled in. Scooby and I had boots on the trail at exactly six thirty, and made tracks for the Skyland Wayside. We made the 4.2 miles in one hour thirty-seven minutes.

Skyland Wayside was beautiful; a full-service restaurant, a fire going in the fireplace, linen tablecloths and napkins—and we walked in looking like the dredges of the earth. They actually sat us on the far side of the dining room. That was okay; there was a breakfast buffet, and they lost money on us because we ate so much. Scooby wanted to get moving (I think to work off his three, full, breakfast plates), and he left the wayside at nine thirty. I waited another fifteen minutes until I saw the rain slow down.

I caught up with him at Byrds Nest 3 Shelter, where we had lunch (a very light lunch). That's when we decided to pound out another twelve miles to the next—and last—wayside in Shenandoah National Park. The wayside closed at five thirty, so we really had to bust out those miles. Yep, we made it there by five, and enjoyed cheeseburgers and fries.

There isn't much to say about the day's hike. It was wet and foggy all day. I felt pretty good about my feet and the new shoes. Sure, they'd gotten soaked, but not as bad as they had gotten soaked in the past. I had them stuffed with paper towels I'd gotten from the wayside, and had new, dry socks to wear in the morning. Unfortunately, it looked like rain again tomorrow.

I was a bit disappointed that I was going to be out of the Shenandoahs soon, and had yet to see a bear. Every squirrel and every chipmunk had me stop dead in my tracks; I just started calling them "baby bears." Scooby had seen a bear—at least he claimed he had. No picture and no scratches/claw marks left it a bit suspect. He did take a picture of where the bear had been; well, there you have it.

I'd noticed these last couple of days that the wild flowers were now really abundant and varied. Splashes of color lined the trail. It was just beautiful. I'd also been seeing a lot of goldfinches; I have always loved that bird.

DAY 69

THE REST OF THE STORY

15.3 Miles Hiked; 964.9 Miles Total
Start: Stealth Camp, Elkwallow Wayside; End: Front Royal Terrapin
Station Hostel

Pez and Glenlivet.

So the rest of the story goes like this: While we—Scooby and I—had been making tracks for Elkwallow Wayside yesterday, Scooby mentioned how awful it would be if the wayside closed at five o'clock. I told him that my guide said it was open for breakfast, lunch, and dinner, from nine in the morning to seven thirty at night. We almost ran to get our burgers and fries. We arrived at five to a sign that read their hours were from nine to five thirty—we'd just made it.

We were cold and very wet, with very limited options for camping anywhere close. I figured that, being a tax payer, they (they, being the park rangers) wouldn't mind if we stealth camped behind the wayside. Actually, "they" *would* mind, so the story I'd come up with as our excuse was this:

"Hello, Mr. Park Ranger. Yes, we are aware that camping here is not permitted. But sir, we were so cold and wet that we felt hypothermia setting in, and we feared for our lives. We knew it would be understood why we camped illegally. Thank you for your understanding." Fortunately, the park rangers had had enough sense to not go out in the rain that night.

In the morning, our plan was to get into Front Royal to the Terrapin Station Hostel, where my sister had sent a drop box that was now waiting for me. Scooby agreed that he could use a night inside, where it was warm and dry, and he agreed to hike there with me.

As we were starting out that morning, Scooby stopped dead in his tracks—and pointed to a bear. Nope, I didn't see it, as I was too busy looking down at my feet. So had Scooby actually seen a bear? No pictures and no scratch/claw marks on him; hmmm, once again, a little suspect.

We arrived by one thirty that afternoon, and showered and took care of laundry by three o'clock. Next, I would go through the drop box I'd gotten from my sister. Susan's mail drop boxes were something I coveted, and would run down the trail for (no wonder I got shin splints).

Inside the box, there were chocolate-covered walnuts, dill pickles, gourmet trail mix, a PEZ dispenser (yes, you read that correctly), a mini bottle of Glenlivet (I love my sister), prepackaged gourmet dinners with recipes included, bacon jerky (touchdown!), macadamia nuts (which she'd sent because of their high fat content), and various other goodies too numerous to mention.

I feel compelled to mention that hiking through Shenandoah National Park was a true pleasure. The trails are beautifully maintained, the way-finding was clear and easy to follow, and the food options at the waysides were greatly appreciated. I, like most thru-hikers, will miss the "Shannies."

Front Royal Terrapin Station Hostel ended up being a pretty good place: a bunk, shower, laundry, frozen pizza and a pop—all for thirty bucks. Mike (the owner) also provided us with a free shuttle into the town of Front Royal. Nobody actually needed a resupply, because everyone had pretty much eaten at the Shenandoah Waysides, leaving us with full food bags. We did accept Mike's recommendation for dinner, though.

PaveMint Taphouse and Grill is an old, converted gas station, now run as a pub that has great food and a terrific beer selection—just what I needed after the terrible weather we had encountered the last couple of days. On the way home from PaveMint, Scooby asked Mike if he would swing by McDonald's for a Big Mac—his second dinner. I got a vanilla ice cream cone. Back at the hostel, we were all warm, safe, and dry while it continued to rain all night.

Day 70

ANOTHER WET AND MUDDY DAY

27.3 Miles Hiked; 992.2 Miles Total
Start: Front Royal Terrapin Station Hostel; End: Rod Hollow Shelter

A Muddy Day.

Scooby and I were up early, with big plans for hiking on toward Harpers Ferry. Our goal was to push on and put down big miles that day. The challenge was that the trail was in awful condition.

To start, it was obvious that we were no longer in Shenandoah National Park, where the trails had been groomed and in ideal shape for the park's visitors. And of course, the rains contributed to poor—and let's just say *unfavorable*—hiking conditions.

Mud the consistency of thick pudding, and rivers/mini lakes on the trail that required us to hop, skip, jump, or just wade through them, made for slow and dangerous hiking. My primary objective was to remain upright, although I failed just once, with a slip and fall in the slick mud. Attempts to keep my shoes and feet dry were futile. It actually got to the point where I marched right through the mess. Honestly, what was going to happen? Once you're soaked, you can't get any wetter. It was actually freeing and liberating to just wade my way through. It was also slow going, though, so we didn't get to our destination until just after eight o'clock that night.

I was so hungry, but also so focused on getting there. The good news was that we only had thirty miles to Harpers Ferry, and would get there early Monday. Scooby had booked a single room for himself in Harpers Ferry before we started hiking together, but was able to call and change it to a double room for us to share.

Harpers Ferry is home to the Appalachian Trail Conservancy, and although it's not the exact halfway point, it tends to, psychologically, be the halfway point. They take your picture when you get there, and give you your new number that designates where you fall among the trail's thru-hikers. I was number 394 when I'd left Georgia, and was anxious to know where I now fell. The Appalachian Trail Conservancy was also where a drop box was waiting for me from another of my dear trail angels (my mother-in-law).

I'd reached a milestone: I'd hiked the most miles I'd ever done in a day: 27.3 miles (Scooby, too). Life was good on the trail.

DAY 71

HIT THE THOUSAND-MILE MARK

21.1 Miles Hiked; 1,013.3 Miles Total
Start: Rod Hollow Shelter; End: David Lesser Memorial Shelter

The David Lesser Memorial Shelter.

Scooby and I had agreed we would get a bit of a later start since we'd gotten in so late the night before. Instead of starting out the next morning at six thirty, we started hiking an hour later.

That day's hike would primarily consist of a fourteen-mile section called "The Roller-coaster," the name it was given due to the constant and repetitive ascents and descents, most of which are extremely steep.

One highlight of the day was when we got to mile number 1,002 and then hiked a short 0.1 miles to the Bears Den Hostel. This property is owned and operated by the Appalachian Trail Conservancy, and is really beautiful. We stopped in for a couple of sodas and chatted with a few thru-hikers who were staying there. If we had timed it right, I know we would have stayed, but we had more miles to go if we were going to meet our daily goal.

When we did arrive at the shelter later that night, we were the only ones there. The shelter was very clean, and had a front porch with a swing. I was going to take my chances and set up in this beautiful shelter, and hope that no one else showed.

Overall, the hike that day had been a very challenging section, with virtually no views worth mentioning, but it was made so much more palatable by having reached the one-thousand-mile mark at the peak of one of those mountains.

We had also achieved another milestone: We had now completed our hike through the state of Virginia, which you may recall makes up 544 miles of the Appalachian Trail. I had now left the fourth of the total fourteen states safely behind me.

We were going to wake up in the morning and start hiking the nine miles into Harpers Ferry. I was really looking forward to achieving this additional milestone, especially because it would only require another short day of hiking.

Day 72

ANOTHER GOAL REALIZED

9.4 Miles Hiked; 1,022.7 Miles Total
Start: David Lesser Memorial Shelter; End: Harpers Ferry, West Virginia

**Whistler Arrives at the Headquarters of the
Appalachian Trail Conservancy.**

We ended up having the shelter to ourselves, and I'd gotten an amazing night of sleep. The next morning, we were up at a quarter past five, and on the trail at six thirty for our 9.4-mile hike into the historic town of Harpers Ferry, West Virginia, home of the Appalachian Trail Conservancy's headquarters.

We would be staying at The Town's Inn, located directly in the center of town and within walking distance—every place is within walking distance for a thru-hiker—of all the local attractions (i.e., *restaurants*).

We arrived around ten that morning, and what a picturesque little town it was. Our first stop was at the headquarters of the Appalachian Trail Conservancy. There, they will take your picture and give you your number indicating your place in that year's "class" of thru-hikers. When I'd begun the journey on March 5 at Amicalola Falls State Park in Georgia, my number had been 394—and now I was number 216.

The folks at the Conservancy's headquarters were remarkable. They were so welcoming and friendly, and really seemed to have a passion for what they do. While we were there, I also picked up a mail drop package that was waiting for me from my mother-in-law. There's really nothing better than receiving a package from family and friends. Thank you for that, Mom!

We checked into our room and then went for lunch, followed by the post office, laundry, and a resupply for "incidentals" (which is code for beer). Oh, by the way, Papa John's delivers.

My only concern was that our inn was very close to the Harpers Ferry train station—a *very active* train station. I didn't have a copy of the train schedule, but five trains had passed in the last two hours. Were they going to be running all night? We would see.

Day 73

Hiking Through Maryland

17.7 Miles Hiked; 1,040.4 Miles Total
Start: Harpers Ferry, West Virginia; End: Dahlgren Backpacker Campground

View from White Rock Cliff.

Yesterday, the heavy train traffic running through Harpers Ferry seemed to go all day and night, and in both directions, but honestly, it was no big deal, as it didn't end up disturbing my sleep (I guess the trains weren't as loud as someone snoring). I have to admit, I had no idea there was so much train activity in the US. All along the trail, and throughout the small towns I'd been through, I had seen and heard more trains than I would have ever expected. It really was almost comforting and nostalgic to see and hear them coming and going.

Scooby and I decided that we would have an early breakfast at seven at The Town's Inn cafe, and then do the short stint of the AT that circles Harpers Ferry. Let me try to explain.

When we had arrived the day before, our main objective had been to get to the Appalachian Trail Conservancy's headquarters. We'd gotten off the trail at the southern end. The trail could be picked up on the northern end through the town, but that would have meant we'd skipped some of the trail. Even though it was the same distance, we were both committed to not skipping a single white blaze. This is a purest approach to hiking the trail, but it was the approach we both agreed to take.

After the short hike, we went back to the inn and ordered sandwiches from a shop across the street that had a bakery, and sold coffee, ice cream, and sandwiches. The person who was working when we got there, Connie, prepared two of the biggest sandwiches I had ever seen. They were placed into our packs, and off we went.

The trail was very kind to us, with limited ascents, but there were a few good miles of foot-bruising rocks that can slow you down. We stopped at Ed Garvey Shelter to eat our sandwiches around one that afternoon, and afterwards, I felt as though I had been put into a food coma. Connie *rocks*!

The rest of our hike took us through and past Gathland State Park, and we saw the beautiful views of White Rock Cliffs. Both of these sites were worthy of having taken breaks for a snack, and were also timely.

In Maryland, you must camp at a designated campsite, which can be at one of their shelters or state run campgrounds. In other words, no stealth camping, which is fine, because they do provide really nice facilities for campers and backpackers.

Our final destination for the evening was Dahlgren Backpacker Campground. This is a Maryland state-run campground, complete with great tentsites, picnic tables, fire rings, and bathrooms with hot showers (I would get a shower two days in a row?). All of that, for no fee. Thank you, Maryland. I wished we would be staying in Maryland longer, but unfortunately, only forty-one miles of the AT runs through this state. Rich in civil war history, and home to the original Washington Monument (which we would see tomorrow), I would definitely revisit Maryland in the future.

My milestone for the day: West Virginia, state number five, was now safely behind me.

DAY 74

IS THIS HEAVEN? BECAUSE I JUST MET AN ANGEL

24.2 Miles Hiked; 1,064.6 Miles Total
Start: Dahlgren Backpacker Campground; End: Falls Creek

Whistler, Washington Monument, Maryland.

Trail angel, Vickie, had made contact with me the next morning via my trail journal guest book. As a section hiker and self-proclaimed trail angel, she had graciously offered to meet me and Scooby to provide us with sub sandwiches and other goodies. She provided trail magic often, and knew where the trail crosses local roads, so coordinating our meeting had been easy.

Vickie brought us Italian subs from her favorite deli, sodas, beers, fresh fruit and brownies she had baked that morning. Thank you, Vickie, for that amazing gift of trail magic, and for your generosity.

It was a tough hike that day, for certain. The rocks were stacked on top of rocks—big rocks, little rocks, and very pointy rocks. From what I'd read, this was just training for what was to come in Pennsylvania. To top it all off, the heat was oppressive. It remained in the mid-eighties all day. It seemed impossible to rehydrate enough.

One of the day's highlights had been stopping that morning at the Washington Monument. This stone tower, dedicated to the father of our country, was built by the townspeople of Boonesboro in 1827. A large group had followed the Stars and Stripes up the mountain on July 4, and started building this impressive monument as part of their Independence Day celebration. Seems a bit more productive than shooting off fireworks, and definitely more patriotic than the fighting that takes place between political parties nowadays. The monument has been restored to its original design, and was certified as a national monument in 1972.

Another highlight was having completed another state. Maryland was now safely behind, and starting tomorrow, I would begin to chip away at the miles in Pennsylvania.

DAY 75

LET ME TELL YOU ABOUT PRINCESS POPPY

23.3 Miles Hiked; 1,087.9 Miles Total
Start: Falls Creek; End: Stealth Camp

Whistler, You Go on Ahead; I'll Catch up Later.

Prior to starting my thru-hike, I'd asked my daughter-in-laws if I could have something that belonged to my grandchildren to take with me. My thoughts were to have something that could photobomb the sights along the way. Sarah provided me with a laminated copy of my favorite picture of my grandson Brantley. Lauren gave me Princess Poppy, which is a shared toy (a troll doll) that belonged to my grand-daughters, Blakely and Katy Ellis. It had been fun and helpful to include my grandchildren a little as I made my journey. Cross from one state to another—photobomb time. A national monument—photobomb. The photo above is another example of Princess Poppy and her shenanigans.

The previous night, we had literally stepped over the Maryland-Pennsylvania border and pitched our tents. It's a psychological head game to be able check off another state. Now all we had to do was hike the 229 miles that made their way through the Keystone State.

Six-thirty, the next morning, was a good time to start. We had targeted doing twelve miles by noon, but had actually achieved thirteen miles by that point (such overachievers). We stopped for lunch at the Rocky Mountain Shelters (yes, plural, as there are twin shelters at each Pennsylvania shelter location—one for snorers and one for non-snorers?)

While there, I looked at my guide and noticed there was a restaurant just over three miles away. Scooby and I had just finished lunch, so it would soon be time for our second lunch. Visions of cold sodas, burgers, and ice cream messed with our sensibilities.

Timbers Restaurant was a short half-mile walk along State Road 30, and was well worth our time and effort. The owner, Wanda, made us feel so welcome. Our glasses of Pepsi never went empty. Our food portions were huge, and the cost was *very* reasonable. Hikers, do not miss this place. There's a charging station, ice cream, great food, and even better prices.

Tomorrow we would arrive at Pine Grove Furnace State Park. Pine Grove, at one time, was the actual halfway mark for the trail, but over time the trail had to be moved, and so was the halfway point. An old-time tradition that exists still is to get a half-gallon of ice cream from the general store there and consume it in a single sitting—halfway, half gallon. Scooby had made that challenge one of his goals for his thru-hike. If you complete the challenge, you get a commemorative wooden spoon (a tiny wooden spoon—wow, right?!). I was still on the fence about whether I would do it.

DAY 76

WHEN IN ROME . . . EAT ICE CREAM?

21.2 Miles Hiked; 1,109.1 Miles Total
Start: Stealth Camp; End: James Fry Shelter

It Really Was So Easy.

I was pretty sure I wouldn't be taking on the half-gallon ice cream challenge. All I can say is that the heat and the miles I'd hiked helped sway my decision-making abilities. It was almost too easy to say yes.

Our hike into Pine Grove Furnace State Park started at a quarter to seven that morning. Scooby liked for me to take the lead, and I found that it kept me moving, knowing he was on my tail. We hit fourteen miles by noon; now that's the power of ice-cream. When we arrived, there was no question as to whether or not I would participate in the ice cream tradition. The only decision to make was what flavor to choose. I went with Neapolitan, and it went down fast. I finished my ice cream in about twenty minutes, and I'd actually beaten Scooby.

Because ice cream now comes in one-and-a-half quart containers, you have to finish an additional container, one with a pint of ice cream, in order to meet the challenge—no problem! Oh, and I got my tiny wooden spoon to prove it.

It's difficult to believe that Pine Grove Furnace State Park, now beautiful, was once home to an iron furnace that dumped byproduct waste into the waters and environment, with no consideration given to the damage it caused. Built in the late eighteenth century using the same methods from four hundred years earlier, this furnace produced iron for our mechanical/industrial age. Hey! That's progress! In addition to the remaining furnace structure, there is now a clean pond for swimming, and a museum and picnic areas. The park is also home to the Appalachian Trail Museum, a must-see for hikers of all ages. I loved a quote from Benton MacKaye (1879-1975), the forester, planner, and conservationist whose idea created the AT, that I'd seen before, and saw once again that day: "The ultimate purpose of the Appalachian Trail? To walk, to see, and to see what you see."

Day 77

WILL THE REAL WHISTLER PLEASE STAND UP?

26.3 Miles Hiked; 1,135.4 Miles Total
Start: James Fry Shelter; End: Darlington Shelter

Whistler Sr. and Whistler Jr.

This was the weekend that the annual Trail Days Festival was held in Damascus, Virginia. The three-day event draws hikers off the trail, and a huge number of alumni, as well. It had been great fun hearing everyone's plans for how they were going to get there. Some of the familiar faces I would see, I hadn't seen yesterday or today, so it was clear they'd gone south. I, myself, couldn't see going backwards to a place I had been weeks ago, and Scooby agreed. We discussed possibly coming back the next year as alumni. We'll see how that goes over with our wives . . .

Scooby and I got off at our usual starting time of six thirty, with plans for a big-miles day. Southern Pennsylvania had been pretty good to us, and the weather had really been cooperating. In fact, that day, it never left the fifties. It was a perfect day for hiking.

One of the pleasures for hikers is that the trail sometimes actually goes straight through, or very close to, a small town. When this occurs, you are compelled and drawn in for a visit. Such an occasion presented itself that day. The trail meanders through the streets of the quaint town of Boiling Springs.

While walking through, we saw small children fishing with grandparents along the shore of the lake in the town center. We saw beautiful public parks and green spaces, a bandstand, and historic buildings with plaques that described their significance to this proud community. The only thing missing was Norman Rockwell and his easel. We stopped and asked for a suggestion for lunch, and were directed to Cafe 101. Holy smokes! The food was incredible.

While we were at the cafe, I chatted a bit with a woman and her young daughter (the husband/father showed up a bit later). After lunch, I asked the woman if she knew of a drug store where I might pick up a knee brace (a twitch had developed in my right knee, and was making me a little concerned). "Sure," she said. "It's a few miles away. I'll drive you there." I was stunned by her gracious and generous response.

My new friend Lou, trail angel, left her husband and daughter at Cafe 101 and shuttled me to the local Rite Aid. From the expression and kind smile on his face, I could tell her husband was accustomed to his wife offering random gifts of kindness. It was that look of pride that said, "Sure, that's my wife. Isn't she awesome?" I know that look, because I wear it all the time when I'm around my wife. How blessed are we to be among angels?

While I was hiking that day, I ran into a young man I had not seen since Damascus. He happened to also go by the trail name "Whistler." How could this be? *I* was Whistler! Well, it's not uncommon to share a trail name. Scooby had learned that there were currently three Scoobys on the trail. Anyway, Whistler Jr. was a nice young man and I enjoyed our banter over who was the original, *true* Whistler (me, by the way).

We hiked for nearly thirteen miles through farm fields, and through wheat that was nearly three feet tall. It was beautifully lush, and although not "amber waves of grain," the wheat *was* a beautiful green, and it did wave in the light breeze. There was corn just coming up in rows that went on for as far as we could see. It was a nice break from the seclusion of the shaded forest we'd become so accustomed to. The surprising thing was how difficult it was to walk for that length of time on flat ground. I actually couldn't wait to climb another mountain.

DAY 78

WELCOME TO ROCKSYLVANIA

15.6 Miles Hiked; 1,151 Miles Total
Start: Darlington Shelter; End: Clarks Ferry Shelter

Whistler at the Doyle Hotel, Duncannon, Pennsylvania.

Our first destination was the small river town of Duncannon, Pennsylvania. We needed to get laundry done, pick up a mail drop, and visit the Doyle Hotel for one of their famous burgers and a cold beer.

The Doyle Hotel is part of the lost Americana of yesteryear. It was obviously a beautiful building in its day, with lots of architectural features you would expect from a turn-of-the-century hotel. Unfortunately, the town of Duncannon has, like so many other small towns, fallen on tough times. It is extremely depressed, and for whatever economy might still exist there, it's not enough to sustain and support such a grand building. It remains a hiker-friendly restaurant and "hotel," but hiker season is just a few months a year. Rooms are twenty-five to thirty-five dollars a night, which is a good value, but you're not getting much for that. My hope is that it can somehow survive, but in the meantime, I was pleased to have been able to enjoy this traditional AT stop while on my journey.

We left Duncannon at two thirty that afternoon, with hopes of adding some miles to the ten it had taken to get to town. Five miles into our hike, the rocks of Pennsylvania revealed themselves, so we stopped. We thought it best to start with fresh legs (and feet) tomorrow. We knew it was coming, but we now knew why hikers call it "Rocksylvania." These rocks have cutting edges on them. We understood that the worst part of Rocksylvania would be northern Pennsylvania. I couldn't wait.

Day 79

I'M BANANAS ABOUT THE AT

28.3 Miles Hiked; 1,179.3 Miles Total
Start: Clarks Ferry Shelter; End: Stealth Camp

Scooby and Whistler, Thousand-Mile Mark.

When we were at Clarks Ferry Shelter the night before, we'd met a terrific young man who went by the trail name "Downhill." We had a great time talking over dinner together, and we'd honestly thought we would leave in the morning with him still asleep. Well, morning came, and Downhill was up and ready to hike with the two old fellows. The weather was perfect, with cloud cover and temperatures in the high fifties and low sixties. The elevations and terrain were perfect for laying down some big miles, so the three of us went at it hard. It was a bit rocky early in the day, but there were clear trails for the better part of the twenty-eight miles we put safely behind us. While crossing over a highway by way of a pedestrian bridge, we did spy trail magic up ahead. Bananas! Thank you, trail angel, who ever you were.

When we finally stopped for the evening, Downhill ate dinner with us, but decided he was too close to having hiked thirty miles that day to quit. He threw his pack on his back and hiked on. Scooby and I—we were satisfied with what we'd achieved.

I'd had a gentleman who had been following me on Trail Journals, and had sent a couple messages via the guestbook. He went by the trail name "Rokk," and he let me know that he would be doing a section hike, and would try to catch up to us. Well, he'd just now found us at around eight o'clock that evening, and he made camp there as well. We would all hike on together tomorrow.

The picture on the previous page was taken by Scooby the day we passed the one-thousand-mile mark on the trail. I failed to get any pictures of us on this particular day, however.

DAY 80

THESE BE HARD ROCKS ON ME FEETS

24.5 Miles Hiked; 1,203.8 Miles Total
Start: Stealth Camp; End: Stealth Camp

Rokk and Whistler at Our Lunchtime Overlook.

Scooby, Rokk and I had boots on the trail at seven that morning. We had a big day ahead of us, with just under twenty-five miles as our goal.

Rokk had done a lot of hiking over the years—but not the same number of miles Scooby and I had put down these last two-plus months. Even still, he was determined to hang with us. He did insist that we go on as we normally would, and if he fell behind, he'd catch up. He would fall behind a bit on the big climbs, but always caught up on the down hills and over the "rock fields" that Pennsylvania is known for. I call the rocks the "great equalizer," because it doesn't matter how strong a hiker you are—everyone goes slow over the rocks.

ROCKSYLVANIA

Welcome to Rocksylvania,
Where the rocks will maim and tame ya.
There's no clear trail,
So you hike on and prevail.
You'll hop and skip,
And quite often trip.
Each step you place
Is slow—not a race!
Rocks both big and small,
And you'll certainly stumble and fall.
They'll tumble and tip,
For your boots, they will rip.
Sure, it's a challenge,
But we all do manage.
For they're in our way,
But that's the price we must pay.
They'll slow down your miles,
So it's best just to smile.

(May, 23rd, 2017, Day 80)

DAY 81

NOW I LAY ME DOWN TO SLEEP (ON A DEFLATED PILLOW)

26.4 Miles Hiked; 1,230.2 Miles Total
Start: Stealth Camp; End: Stealth Camp

**Whistler and Scooby with Donald Gauntlett,
Trail Angel, of Tremont, Pennsylvania.**

We hiked thirteen miles into Port Clinton by eleven thirty (Rokk was a bit behind, and had not yet arrived). This little sleepy town is home to a pretty large train yard, but the town is obviously a bit depressed. The census report online showed a dramatic decrease in population. It's a cute little town, and one worth visiting if you happen to be hiking or driving through. I understand that coal mining is still a major economic driver for the area, and still provides jobs and keeps the trains that run through the town very productive. David "Awol" Miller's book, *The AT Guide: A Handbook for Hiking the Appalachian Trail*, mentions the Peanut Store, which to me, is code for "snacks."

When we entered the store, we found ourselves in a total state of shock. This store is practically in the middle of nowhere, but was full, floor to ceiling, with every candy you could ever imagine. We were like kids in a candy store (literally). The clerk, Kate, told us that people will drive from as far as Philadelphia to get their favorite candy. Their best seller is their fresh-roasted peanuts.

After we had satisfied our sweet tooth, we walked next door to the Port Clinton Hotel for lunch. Scooby and I had ordered our lunch when Rokk finally arrived, along with another gentleman named Don. Don was in his seventies, and he had been offering trail magic when he'd met Rokk. Rokk decided he was going to buy Don lunch to show his appreciation. Rokk didn't stop there, either. He insisted on buying my lunch, and Scooby's, as well. Incidentally, the food at this place was off-the-charts good. The hamburger was probably one of the best on the trail.

Rokk's two days of hiking with us were over, and his wife Peggy was on her way to pick him up. He admitted it had been tough to keep up with us, but personally, I was impressed with how well he had kept up—a real trooper, great trail angel, and fun to be around. Thank you, Rokk for spending a couple days on the trail with us.

After lunch, Don took us to his car and loaded us up with more trail magic: snacks, drinks, and cheese. We were all set to knock off another thirteen miles.

If you'll remember, I had broken one of my trekking poles on Blood Mountain. After coming off Blood Mountain, you come to Mountain Crossings outfitters at Neel Gap. The clerk there had told me that my broken pole was under warranty by the manufacturer. My response was, "Why would I do that?" The pole hadn't been defective; I'd fallen and broken it—not their fault. I'm giving this background information to set up the next story.

I'd gotten a special treat for myself, which was the purchase of my Sea to Summit blow-up pillow. It had cost me around forty-five dollars, but was well worth it for my sleeping comfort. A few weeks ago, I had noticed it was leaking. Most recently, I was having to blow it up six to eight times a night. I decided that I needed it to be replaced by Sea To Summit. All I did was put my head on it each night (what you'd expect, right?). Annie had all the purchase info at home, so I asked her to reach out to them.

After a number of calls and emails, the associate at Sea to Summit—Jacob—sent me an email that asked me to take the pillow, inflate it, place the pillow in a basin of water, take a picture of where the bubbles were coming from, and then email the picture of the air bubbles to him. Not a joke—he was serious. For the record, he knew I was on the trail as a thru-hiker (highly unlikely that I would have a basin in my backpack). So I called again from somewhere along mile marker 1,200 on the AT, which was in the middle of nowhere. This time the person who answered the phone—Brie—listened to me (key word, *listened*), and agreed they needed to get me a new pillow. A short time later, I got an email from Jacob: a new pillow was en route.

I was going to be off the trail for five days, starting the upcoming Friday, to attend my niece's high school graduation. Annie and I are actually honorary aunt and uncle to Ashley, who we've known and loved since before she was born. I would also have a couple days to see my sons and their families, as well. Scooby was going to continue hiking for two more days. Then he, too, would be off the trail. He and his wife were going to be taking a five-day vacation. I was going to come back two days before his return, catch up to where he'd gone off the trail, and then continue with him once he got back.

DAY 82

THOSE ROCKS ARE SLIPPERY WHEN WET

13.7 Miles Hiked; 1,243.9 Miles Total
Start: Stealth Camp; End: Blue Mountain Summit Bed & Breakfast

Whistler, the Pinnacle.

Scooby and I had agreed on a departure time of around seven the next morning, after having hiked so hard and late the day before. When I woke at four to the sound of heavy rain, I just knew it was going to be ugly. My best defence was to roll over and go back to sleep. When I was up and about, I prepared my instant grits (which I hate but fills the stomach), and waited for either the rain to slow or stop, or for Scooby to start making some positive movements. When neither happened, I just pulled it together and packed up. We were both eventually ready to go, and hit the trail by a quarter past seven.

The thirteen miles we needed to do would have—and should—have been easy, but the rain made them miserable. Climbing over rocks the size of basketballs, up to the size of small cars is tough enough, but add the element of rain and it becomes doubly tough. Scooby fell first, and I followed suit. The rocks themselves are rough, but add water and they can get crazy slippery. My hands and feet had turned into shrivelled prunes, and I was losing feeling in my fingers. I was so cold that my teeth were chattering (and we call this "fun"?). At one point, there was a break in the rain, and I let Scooby know that I had to eat something; I needed fuel. Two minutes after a quick snack it was pouring again.

We finally came to a break in the rocks, and I found myself running, with Scooby right on my heels. It felt good to make up some time and miles after the slow crawls over those stinking rocks. Earlier, we had figured it would be around two in the afternoon before we arrived at our bed and breakfast, Blue Mountain Summit—the running got us there at twelve thirty. In our room after a hot shower, now dressed in warm clothes, we were ready for burgers and beer.

Enterprise was going to pick me up early the next morning, and then I would be on the road to my son's home in Lexington, South Carolina. Life was so good.

The picture of me on the previous page, at the "pinnacle," had actually been taken the day before. The only views I'd seen today were of rain, on top of more rain.

DAY 83

I'LL BE BACK

0 Miles Hiked; 1,243.9 Miles Total
Start: Blue Mountain Summit Bed & Breakfast; End: Off trail

Dinner Upon Arrival.

I was up at five thirty, even with having been in a comfortable bed in a clean, warm room. Scooby and I were ready to hike that morning—but I wasn't going anywhere. We had a great breakfast at our B&B, and washed it all down with plenty of fresh coffee. I was waiting on the person from Enterprise to pick me up, while Scooby was ready to hike on. It felt really strange for me to watch him go while I stayed behind. The good news was that he'd run reconnaissance for me and provide me with hiking data; not that it would really matter, because it was what it was. I just liked knowing what was up ahead.

I was really excited to know that I was going to see my sons and their beautiful families. Just thinking about them, brought me true joy, and real tears to my eyes. My only wish was that I could see Annie, as well. For that, I would have to get back on the trail and move my little legs as fast as I could.

DAY 84

HOW BLESSED WE ARE

0 Miles Hiked; 1,243.9 Miles Total
Start: Off trail; End: Off trail

Whistler and Ashley, the Graduate.

I really didn't know what to say. I'd known this young lady since before she was born, and that day I was watching her walk across a stage to accept her high school diploma. How did that happen? It was an honor to see Ashley accept her just reward for all her hard work, but the greatest honor was to be present as part of her family. Her father, Steve, is like a brother to me, and her mother, Barbie, is so dear to me.

I could remember the Mother's Day at church when they announced that Barbie was pregnant. They had tried to have children for twelve years by that point, and had given up hope. The Lord obviously had big plans for them though, and blessed them with Ashley. Steve and Barbie are also honorary aunt and uncle to our boys. They led the youth Sunday school class for our oldest son, Richard. We've shared so many family celebrations together that it was just natural for me to be there for Ashley's graduation.

Ashley would be attending Columbia College on a swimming scholarship, which she had earned through hard work and perseverance. That she would achieve that, was not surprising at all when you know how she was raised. God has blessed Steve and Barbie with this little girl, and Annie and I have been blessed to watch her grow into the beautiful person she is today. We are truly blessed!

DAY 85

FOR THE LOVE OF FAMILY

0 Miles Hiked; 1,243.9 Miles Total
Start: Off trail; End: Off trail

Brian, Sarah, Harrison, Grandpop Whistler, and Brantley.

It was going to be another wonderful day. I woke up a bit late, as the after-graduation celebrations at the Sawyer house had continued late into the evening. When we were all up, Steve made his typical breakfast, which is usually enough for the whole neighborhood. After breakfast, I said my goodbyes, and made off to see my son Brian and his family in North Charleston.

Our plan was to grab lunch together, but believe it or not, I wasn't that hungry. I'm not sure if that was because I hadn't hiked for a couple of days, or if I was still full from Steve's huge breakfast. We went to a local hamburger joint called Sesame, and I skipped the burger and had a salad. After lunch, we went back to their home, hung out, and caught up a bit. I was back on the road and heading for Lexington by mid-afternoon. It was such a blessing to have spent time with my family.

I would be meeting a friend for coffee in the morning, and spending the rest of the day with my son Richard. He and I were going to enjoy our favorite pub for lunch, have a couple beers, and then see a movie.

Boy, was I ever going to miss this time I'd had with my family.

DAY 86

TIME TO HEAD BACK TO THE TRAIL

0 Miles Hiked; 1,243.9 Miles Total
Start: Off trail; End: Off trail

Grandpop Whistler, Blakely, Katy Ellis, Richard, and Lauren.

The day started a bit early, as I had made plans to meet with a colleague/friend who I had not seen in the ten years since I had retired. Phil had most recently retired from working for Publix Supermarkets, and now he and his wife Vonnie were building a home there in Lexington. He and I met that morning over coffee, and we caught up as best we could in the one and a half hours we spent together.

We parted with the promise to see each other over the holidays, when Annie and I would be back to visit our family.

The rest of this glorious day was mostly spent with my son Richard. We ran a couple of errands, had lunch, and caught that movie together. Once we got home, I started getting my gear together, and packed for my early morning departure and the nearly seven-hundred-mile drive back to Pennsylvania. It had been a great visit. My daughter-in-law, Lauren, fed me as if on a personal mission to put some weight back on my bones. She and my granddaughters baked brownies and cookies for me. I did my best to show my appreciation the best way I know how: I ate like a starving hiker, but left just enough for them.

DAY 87

WELCOME BACK, WHISTLER

5.9 Miles Hiked; 1,249.8 Miles Total
Start: Blue Mountain Summit Bed & Breakfast; End: Bake Oven
Knob Shelter

One of the Day's Rock Climbs Over My Shoulder.

Knowing that I had a 650-mile drive this morning motivated me to
have everything packed and ready to go the night before. I had the
pleasure of saying goodnight to my granddaughters, and then sat up
a bit talking with Richard and Lauren. I was up at four thirty the next
morning, and backing out of the driveway an hour later. The drive itself was long—650 miles and eleven hours—but thankfully uneventful.
I arrived at Enterprise just after four that afternoon and they had me
back to the trailhead just before five. It's funny how I'd gotten off the
trail that last Thursday with Scooby, in the pouring rain, and it looked
like it had never stopped. I wanted to get a few miles behind me, so I
did 5.9 to the Bake Oven Knob Shelter.

It was slow going for the rain, and there were some really big rock climbs—slippery, wet rock climbs. It was looking like there would be similar weather tomorrow, but I really needed to lay down some miles. I was meeting Scooby at Delaware Water Gap on Thursday night, so I needed to do forty-four more miles in the next two days. I was up for it.

DAY 88

BEAR!

26.8 Miles Hiked; 1,276.6 Miles Total
Start: Bake Oven Knob Shelter; End: Stealth Camp

My First Bear Sighting.

It was one of those days that was so full that I hope I can remember everything.

I started early, knowing that I wanted to lay down some big miles. I was just about a mile out of camp when I came up on a woman who seemed happy to see me. Her trail name was Energizer, and apparently she wasn't sure if she was going north on the trail or not. She told me that the rocks "all looked familiar." I'll second that. I assured her that she was indeed heading north.

The rain that morning made for very difficult hiking, especially since I was hiking some of the most difficult terrain I had experienced yet. The climb out of Lehigh Gap is a vertical, rock-and-boulder climb that requires two hands and two feet—no place here for trekking poles. This mountainside is a deforested ridge left over from the days of zinc smelting that occurred between 1898 and 1980. It's not the prettiest mountain, but it was a fun, challenging climb.

My reward for the climb was twofold. The first of my rewards was trail magic that was left by Grace—trail name, Earthling. Grace was a 2015 thru-hiker alumna, and was out for a day hike. The second of my rewards: my first bear sighting. It had just stopped raining, and I had just finished my big climb, when I started hiking the ridge. I came up and over a hump and saw the bear on the trail walking towards me. As soon as he saw me, he turned and started to run on all fours.

I was afraid I wouldn't be able to get my phone out of the Ziploc bag fast enough to get a picture. I started running after him (or was it a her?) to help ensure a picture as proof of my sighting. That's when he stopped, turned to face me, and got on his hind legs. I swear it looked as though he realized it was just me. It looked as though he was getting ready to ask, "Is that you, Whistler? I almost didn't recognize you." I got my pictures, and he turned and ran off. I was so excited I felt like a child, but I didn't care. The first thing I did was call Annie. I think she thought I had been attacked by the bear. The next thing I did was send the picture to Scooby.

A short time later I met Jem. Jem was a section hiker who had done well over half the trail, and was a pleasure to speak with. I sat down where she had been resting and made myself some lunch. When I told her my name, she told me she had seen and read my journal. Apparently her mother read it, as well. She sent her mom a text, and her mom replied, asking if I had my granddaughters' troll. I pulled Princess Poppy out and Jem took a picture of me with Poppy to send to her mother. Jem's mother also wanted to know where Scooby was—a small world.

Speaking of Scooby, I was going to be meeting him in Delaware Water Gap tomorrow afternoon. We would start hiking together on Friday, but I thought we might have to have a couple of beers together and catch up first.

DAY 89

PENNSYLVANIA, SEE YA

16.7 Miles Hiked; 1,293.3 Miles Total
Start: Stealth Camp; End: Presbyterian Church of the Mountain

Live Jazz at the Deer Head Inn.

Pennsylvania, Pennsylvania, Pennsylvania. It's not that the rocks were so bad—even though they really were—it's just that the rocks never end. It's as though they dig holes and plant the rocks, pointy tips up. Rumor has it that they sneak out after hikers are sleeping soundly in their tents, and file the rocks to make sure they keep their boot-penetrating edges.

The good news was that we would exit Pennsylvania tomorrow and enter The Garden State. My vision was to cross that border, take my shoes off, and hike barefoot to Mount Katahdin. We would see whether my vision would become anywhere close to reality.

Scooby and I caught up with each other exactly as planned. I got to meet "Mrs. Scooby," as well (an added bonus). After making a resupply run to Wal-Mart, we returned to the Presbyterian Church of the Mountain. This church has, as part of their outreach, a hiker feed every Thursday night (perfect timing). There had to be forty of us hikers, and I promise you that none of us left hungry.

After dinner I got word there was live jazz at the Deer Head Inn next to the church. Could it get any better? I sent Scooby a text and told him the aforementioned info, and he was quick to get dressed for the occasion. In all, eight of the usual suspects (thru-hikers) joined us for beers and jazz. A perfect send-off before we happily exited Pennsylvania.

DAY 90

WHAT A DIFFERENCE A STATE MAKES

24.9 Miles Hiked; 1,318.2 Miles Total
Start: Presbyterian Church of the Mountain End: Brink Road Shelter

Pennsylvania, Left Safely Behind Us.

What an absolutely beautiful day we had—a day made just for hiking. We left the Church of the Mountain at seven that morning; a bit later than we would have normally left because we'd stayed a bit late at the Deer Head Inn the evening before. The beer was cold and the jazz was hot. Delaware Water Gap sure had a lot of talent for such a small community, and the Deer Head Inn was a great little venue to showcase these great musicians. We crossed over the Delaware River, and halfway across was the Pennsylvania-New Jersey border. That was seven states down, and seven more to go.

It was simply unbelievable how the terrain changed from one state (Pennsylvania) to another (New Jersey). Sure, there were still some rocky areas, but nothing close to the misery of the rocks in Pennsylvania. Our hike took us to several beautiful vistas that day, including Sunfish Pond. This pond is a forty-four-acre glacier lake formed during the last ice age, and was recognized as a national natural landmark in 1970. It is stunningly beautiful, and was especially so because we just hadn't seen too many bodies of water in the mountains thus far. It was difficult to take your eyes off it while hiking along the pond's shore. I also stepped right over a rattlesnake that day, as well; a short fellow of about two feet. Scooby saw it just before he, too, almost stepped on it but managed to step over it.

We took a break that afternoon on top of Rattlesnake Mountain (ironic, right?). The views of the Delaware River Valley and the Poconos Mountains were vast. It was amazing how far you could see when it wasn't raining or foggy.

DAY 91

ALL ABOARD

26.7 Miles Hiked; 1,344.9 Miles Total
Start: Brink Road Shelter; End: Unionville, New York

Scooby and Train Wreck on the Marsh Boards.

Our vision for that morning involved us getting breakfast in Branchville, New Jersey—except every place apart from the local bait shop was closed. I'd seriously thought about some bait/shiners on a tortilla, but settled for a cold Pepsi to wash down a couple of Pop-Tarts I had in my food bag.

Our primary goal for that day was to hike into Unionville, which happens to be in New York. Confused yet? Yep, me too. New Jersey and New York share the area that hugs the AT. This is similar to how North Carolina and Tennessee share the AT—one foot in, one foot out. Anyway, while in Unionville, New York, what else would you expect a thru-hiker to do but eat New York-style pizza for dinner? There is a reason why New York has their reputation for good pizza. They actually earn it. Yes, Unionville is a small town, but it is a hiker-friendly town. They allow thru-hikers to camp at the local park. The only thing required is that you register—and you do that at the local grocery store. I love small towns.

There seemed to be an addition to the Whistler-Scooby northbound train to Mount Katahdin. A thru-hiker named Train Wreck joined us, and was a good addition to our trek. A seemingly nice guy from Alabama, he'd recently retired from thirty-plus years with the railroad. Train Wreck kept pace with us young fellows. He'd actually started his thru hike on March 23, had only had three zeros, and at sixty-one years old, he was a hiking machine who would challenge us every step of the way. I love a challenge.

DAY 92

AND I'M CLIMBING A STAIRWAY TO HEAVEN

16.8 Miles Hiked; 1,361.7 Miles Total
Start: Unionville, New York; End: Wawayanda Shelter

Fresh New York Baked Goods at Horler's General Store.

The town of Unionville, New York is one of those towns that seems to be stuck in a time warp. I say this lovingly, and with so much envy. This is one of those small American towns where "Old Glory" flies proudly on every telephone pole and in every yard, and red, white and blue bunting billows below windows along main street as though the parade shall pass at any moment.

We'd eaten our pizza on the front porch of the local pizzeria last night. After dinner, we walked across the street to our tents in the local park. We agreed that we would get a late start the next day because we wanted a big breakfast at the local grocery store called Horler's General Store.

This little store opened at seven the next morning, and we found ourselves standing in line to place our orders. They had genuine, New York-style bagels, and doughnuts that were out of this world. Scooby ate seven of the doughnuts that were the size of tea cup saucers. Train Wreck had just two. I had an everything bagel with egg, cheese, and Taylor ham on it, and two filled doughnuts. We each also ordered subs to go in our packs for lunch later. We all agreed that the subs must have had a pound of meat stacked on the rolls. I love New York!

We were again in and out of New Jersey and New York all day. We would cross from New Jersey and into New York for the last time tomorrow.

Our hike took us over a boardwalk that crosses you over a marsh. This boardwalk is just under a mile long, and includes a suspension bridge that takes you over Pochuck Creek. Building these structures had to have been a monumental task, and it sure made our hiking through that area a pleasure.

Immediately after we finished that section, we started our steep, rocky, and nearly one thousand-foot climb up the "Stairway to Heaven"—a great challenge and a great way to work off our lunch.

We made it an early and short day, both because we had gotten a late start and because we'd spent the last half of the day hiking in rain. The plan for tomorrow was to start early and hike close to twenty-eight miles. Unfortunately, it looked liked rain all day. I hated when that happened!

WHAT'S YOUR (TRAIL) NAME?

We come here from far and wide,
With hopes and dreams to abide.
You leave your given name behind.
A new one that fits, you hope to find.
Slips and falls are all you've got?
Congratulations, "Sir Falls-a-Lot."
The weight you carry has you bragging.
Now you're known as "Chuckwagon."
Listening to tunes as you go?
Your brand new name is "Radio."
It's all in fun, and what we do,
Come and join us! We'll name you, too.

(June, 4th, 2017, Day 92)

DAY 93

GOODBYE, GARDEN STATE; HELLO, BIG APPLE

22.5 Miles Hiked; 1,384.2 Miles Total
Start: Wawayanda Shelter; End: Stealth Camp

New Jersey, Safely Behind Us.

When we'd arrived at the Wawayanda Shelter last night, it had just been the three of us, so I thought I'd take my chances in the shelter alongside Train Wreck. Scooby had decided he'd rather sleep in his tent. My objective was to avoid setting up and taking my tent down in the rain. Well, it had rained like crazy, and I was happy with my decision.

We decided to get an early start the next morning, so we began the day at six. We passed the New Jersey-New York border, and left New Jersey safely behind us. That was eight states down, and six to go. Our plan was to hike twenty-six miles, but it just didn't work out. The hiking that day was some of the toughest we'd experienced thus far.

I had an especially difficult day. I slipped and fell a couple of times on some of the steep declines. One of my falls was actually the deciding factor to end our day prior to having achieved our twenty-six-mile goal. I had started taking some missteps, and had asked Train Wreck to take the lead. He managed to take a steep decline with relative ease, but I slipped, hopped, skipped, and jumped, while nearly causing myself serious harm. I landed on my feet, but with a huge rock uncomfortably between my legs, and dangerously close to my knees—so close, I would say it was nearly "hike-ending."

With my heart pounding, I took a quick inventory and realized how blessed I was that the Good Lord was watching over me. I looked ahead and took notice when Train Wreck glanced back at me with what appeared to be a lack of concern; he then turned back around and hiked on. Meanwhile, Scooby came up behind me with genuine concern. Scooby had witnessed my acrobatic feat and understood how close I had come to serious injury. It was then that he called out to Train Wreck and suggested we call it a day. It was getting dark, and was also raining, and I for one was ridiculously tired—a recipe for disaster.

New York had certainly been challenging, to say the least. I was looking forward to a fresh start in the morning. Today had also been a big day for mosquitoes; they had been searching for some trail magic of their own—in the form of a Whistler-type-O blood feast. I finally had to break out the DEET insect repellant that I had carried with me since Springer Mountain.

The highlight of our day had to be the ice cream we got at Bellvalle Farms Creamery. It didn't come as a surprise to us when we learned that this ice cream shop was rated number two in the entire United States, according to TripAdvisor. I had a two-scoop ice cream sundae, while both Scooby and Train Wreck had banana splits, followed up with milk shakes.

DAY 94

SQUEEZE ME TENDER

18.7 Miles Hiked; 1,402.9 Miles Total
Start: Stealth Camp; End: Bear Mountain Inn

Whistler's Turn through the Lemon Squeezer.

We awoke and sat in our tents to the sounds of heavy rain, but our patience paid off, as a pause in the precipitation allowed us to make a break for it. The night before, I was so tired and frustrated that I don't think I could have gone any further. I don't want to sound overly dramatic, but I had nearly taken what could have been a hike-ending spill. Fortunately, my hiking partners had both been in agreement that we needed to call it quits. Our hike the next morning would prove that it would have been past nine o'clock before we would have arrived at our targeted stopping point, anyway—validating that we'd made the correct decision.

Our hiking itinerary the next day was to hit the trail at six thirty, and hopefully make up the miles we'd lost last night. Reaching an iconic landmark on the trail called the "Lemon Squeezer" was one of our early morning challenges. The Lemon Squeezer is an outcropping of two huge boulders that sit at a precarious angle, which requires you to manipulate yourself to pass through. Some hikers actually have to remove their backpacks to "squeeze" through.

We eventually came to Arden Valley Road in the late morning, and recalled that there was a state park two-tenths of a mile off the trail, and our trail guides indicated that that park had vending machines. When we arrived, we found vending machines with candy, soda, and ice cream and—wait, it gets better—the machines accepted credit cards (I love technology). It ended up being a very lucrative stop for the park as a huge deposit made its way to their bank account thanks to three starving hikers.

With bellies full, we marched right back to the trailhead and hit it in serious fashion—that is, until we got hungry and started planning our next feeding. Careful consideration and planning went into this collective thought process. As it turned out, we discovered that between the three of us, we actually had one complete brain. The plan was to hike to Bear Mountain Inn, share a room (which, split three ways, is a pretty good deal), order local New York pizza, and enjoy it while sitting in the hotel bar. So it turned out that our collective brain was somewhere around genius level.

DAY 95

WHAT'S WITH ALL THESE STONE WALLS?

26.1 Miles Hiked; 1,429 Miles Total
Start: Bear Mountain Inn; End: RPH Shelter

One of Many Stone Walls in New York.

The Bear Mountain Inn is a beautiful and historic property. Built in 1915, it has long been a popular escape for New York City dwellers. The inn was so nice, in fact, that the three of us agreed we wouldn't hang our tents on the furniture in the room to dry them out. Unfortunately, the room did take on the odor of three thru-hikers. This smell can only be compared to that of a wet St. Bernard. The room would possibly need to be fumigated or removed from the hotel inventory for the rest of the season.

The three pizzas we had delivered and enjoyed for dinner helped further substantiate the fact that New York has the best pizza in the world—hands down!

The next morning, we left the comfort of our hotel room and made our way back to the trail by seven.

A notable landmark is the Bear Mountain Trailside Museum and Zoo. The AT passes directly through the zoo, which also happens to be the lowest point in elevation (124 feet above sea level) on the 2,200-mile trek. Unfortunately, we arrived way too early before their opening time of ten thirty, and we were required to take the blue-blazed trail around. We made up for our disappointment by hiking the six miles to the Appalachian deli/convenience store for breakfast and to-go subs for our lunch later. Oh, and ice cream sandwiches were squeezed in after breakfast, too.

We had seen these old, dry-stacked stone walls throughout the forests we had hiked these last several days in New York. I knew nothing of their origins, but we all took several guesses. Had they been built to delineate old property lines? Or perhaps to keep in grazing animals? Who had built them? How had they built them, and why? One suggestion I had was for Pennsylvania to come see what New York had done with their rocks—perhaps Pennsylvania could learn a thing or two.

Later, we ran into a couple of guys we'd met the day before when they were trail running. We crossed paths with them at a crossroad where they were meeting with their friend and shuttle driver. Trail magic flowed our way in the form of cold Coca-Colas and cookies.

DAY 96

DOVER OAK, WITH SOME TRAIL MAGIC ON THE SIDE

25.6 Miles Hiked; 1,454.6 Miles Total
Start: RPH Shelter; End: Wiley Shelter

Standing at the Base of Dover Oak.

Ralph's Peak Hikers' Cabin, better known as RPH Shelter, had been a great stopping point the night before. It's a unique shelter, and was once a private cabin that has since been converted to an AT shelter. It is located in the middle of a neighborhood, and has a great big lawn area that was perfect for tenting. Although we didn't take advantage of restaurant delivery, several other hikers had pizza and Chinese food delivered. We made our plans to start hiking the next morning by six thirty, and said our good nights.

Morning came and we were on the trail by six thirty, as planned. We hiked about five miles and came to another crossroad with a deli just three-tenths of a mile off trail—time to take a detour.

After a breakfast sandwich, coffee, and some ice cream, we made our way back to the trail. We all agreed that we would miss the accessibility of great food so close to the trail that the narrow corridor through New York offered. In the meantime, we were taking full advantage.

We later met Story Time, an alumni member of the 2013 class of AT thru-hikers. He was out on a day hike, and stopped to chat with us about our hike. He was quick to open his pack and share its contents: trail magic!

A short distance later, we had arrived at the Dover Oak. This beautiful tree, estimated to be over three hundred years old, is twenty-two feet in circumference and known as the largest oak on the trail. While taking advantage of the photo opportunity afforded by the Dover Oak, Story Time then showed up to get his car. Prior to driving off, he came back to give us yet more trail magic. Thank you, Story Time, for understanding how much trail magic means to a thru-hiker.

Just before seven o'clock that evening, we stopped for the day at Wiley Shelter. We made camp, ate, hung our food bags up, and crawled into our tents. It had been another great day of hiking, but we were beat.

DAY 97

I LOVE NEW YORK ... CONNECTICUT, TOO

22.8 Miles Hiked; 1,477.4 Miles Total
Start: Wiley Shelter; End: Silver Hill Campsite

Ready to Knock Off the Next State.

I knew it was going to be another glorious day when the sun lit up my tent with an early morning glow. In addition to that, the dew levels were down, and I got to pack a dry tent—less weight. We left Wiley Shelter that morning at seven (yep, we slept in an additional thirty minutes yippee!), and 1.5 miles later, we crossed the New York-Connecticut border. We had officially entered New England, and New York was now in our rearview mirrors.

Honestly, New York was fantastic to hike through. The people were wonderful and the food that was accessible to us was amazing. The funny thing is that these mountains are so close to populated areas that we were almost always within earshot of a highway and close to convenience stores, delis, and of course, New York-style pizza. You really can't help but take advantage of these opportunities, because they are otherwise pretty rare occurrences, and they mean so much to a thru-hiker.

One of the local sites we'd all agreed was a must-see was Bull's Bridge. This covered bridge dates back to the eighteen hundreds, and has been lovingly maintained. It was well worth the six-tenths of a mile off trail it took to see. The added bonus was the Bull's Bridge convenience store, where we had our second breakfast, coffee, and ice cream, and packed out sandwiches for lunch. Like I said, you just can't pass up those opportunities.

We continued on, and we hiked along the beautiful Housatonic River for well over a mile.

We had a number of big climbs, as well. I think they were exceedingly difficult because of how tired we all were. We kept getting up early and hiking late. Most days had involved eleven to twelve hours of hiking, anywhere from twenty-two to twenty-eight miles. By the end of the day, we were dragging ourselves to our planned stopping point. We were making the best of the journey, but I think we were also ready to finish up.

One particular descent, called St. John's Ledges, was exceedingly difficult on its own, but that in addition to how tired we were made it take twice as long as it should have. Scooby was getting shin splints; my knees and shins hurt; and Train Wreck had sore feet (actually, we all did). It was time to take a nero.

We would pull into Salisbury tomorrow, where Scooby and I had resupplies waiting (and I was also expecting new shoes), and check into a hostel, do laundry, take much-needed showers, and eat some (and eat some more again). The plan was to get a big breakfast on Sunday and put in a shorter day, mileage wise—that was the plan, anyway.

DAY 98

MARCHING TO SALISBURY, CONNECTICUT

22.5 Miles Hiked; 1,499.9 Miles Total
Start: Silver Hill Campsite; End: Vanessa Breton's Hostel

Can It Really Be This Beautiful?

Our plan for the day was to hit the trail at six thirty and then make our way to Salisbury. We had a few big climbs in the morning, but we hiked like there was a prize waiting for us at the end of day—because there was. Our hostel was run by a lovely woman, Vanessa Breton. Scooby, Train Wreck, and myself, along with a young man named Honey Bagder we'd been leapfrogging, took over the entire bunk room.

Although there was the opportunity to go off trail for what Train Wreck called "hiker kibble," we all agreed to ignore the temptation and march on to Salisbury.

THE MOUNTAINS

Their beauty makes its daily call,
That hikers answer with their all.
They reach for heaven and touch the sky.
Our goal to conquer, but we don't know why.
It starts each morning with first light,
And lasts all day till twilight.
The challenge changes day by day.
"Is that all you've got?" is what we say.
Our bodies hardened by what we do,
The aches and pains stay with us, too.
It's not a game or a race.
It's about getting to that sacred place.
We all march toward that last sunrise.
That day will come, and so will the prize.

(June, 10th, 2017, Day 98)

DAY 99

GOODBYE, MY FRIEND—AT LEAST FOR NOW

13.4 Miles Hiked; 1,513.3 Miles Total
Start: Vanessa Breton's Hostel; End: Glen Brook Shelter

View from Mount Everett.

You may recall the point in the journey when I'd just returned to the trail after taking eight days off to allow my feet and shins to heal. I had lost several toenails, and had some serious shin-splint issues. When I'd gotten back to the trail, I had hiked a few miles when I came to a forestry road that crossed the AT; that's when I'd spotted the guy sitting on a stone wall, eating a bag of chocolate donuts. I'd waved politely and asked if he was okay. If you remember, I started to hike on, but then thought I should turn back around and introduce myself. Scooby and I had now hiked about 650 miles since that chance meeting.

Let me stress that it is extremely difficult to find someone you can hike with. Different personalities, hiking speeds, and just different thoughts on how to achieve common goals make for a cautious approach when deciding whether to commit to hiking with someone. Well, my friend and hiking partner had been fighting serious shin splints for over a week now, and had wisely decided to take a zero (possibly more) and then reduce his daily miles. I told him that I'd take some time off with him, but he selflessly insisted I continue. I was certain that Scooby was going to finish his hike, but unfortunately it appeared we wouldn't summit Mount Katahdin together.

Train Wreck and I had a big breakfast with Scooby that morning, and I said my goodbyes. I'm not going to lie. It was difficult. It was like saying goodbye to a brother.

On the trail by ten, which was late for us, we agreed to have a short day of thirteen-plus miles.

A couple of the climbs ended up being really tough. Bear Mountain was (yep, another Bear Mountain), for one, but Mount Everett really kicked our butts. Our plan for tomorrow was to start hiking by six to take advantage of the early light and cooler temperatures.

Train Wreck and I had exited Connecticut and entered Massachusetts. That was ten states down and four to go.

We had also passed the 1,500-mile mark. I called and spoke with Scooby that evening once Train Wreck and I had arrived at our planned camp. He was in good spirits. That was just like him; it's who he is.

Day 100

BABY, IT'S HOT OUT HERE

21.4 Miles Hiked; 1,534.7 Miles Total
Start: Glen Brook Shelter; End: Mount Wilcox North Shelter

Leaving Connecticut; Entering Massachusetts.

As planned, Train Wreck and I were hiking by six the next morning. We met at the picnic table for coffee and conversation with a couple of other flip-flop thru-hikers, and then made our way up the trail. A flip-flop hiker is one that will start at a point along the trail (usually close to the middle such as Harpers Ferry) hike north to Mt. Katahdin, get a ride back to their starting point and hike south to Springer Mountain. This is one example of a flip-flop hike but there is no defined starting or ending point. A hiker will take this approach if they are perhaps starting late in the season and perhaps concerned about a late summit at Katahdin not being possible due to Baxter State Park closing in mid October.

The trail ran its way through a beautiful conifer forest for a good part of the day. The trail was soft underfoot for all the pine needles. Unfortunately, the overall trail conditions were poor, at best. Heavy growth hanging over the trail made passage difficult at times. A lot of washouts told a story of neglect, as well. I know all of us thru-hikers appreciate the efforts of those who work hard to maintain the trail, and we always thank any of these people we meet on the trail. My criticism was simply an observation, and a fair comparison to the trails in those states we'd already hiked. We could only assume that the trail club responsible was having some trouble with getting volunteers.

I know I've already mentioned the personal cravings I'd had while hiking, but lately, I simply couldn't get enough cold Coca-Cola. We crossed US 7 and walked to an antique store that had cold sodas. I sucked down two Cokes in about three minutes. The oppressive heat had made it impossible to get enough fluids, but it looked like the forecast was predicting some cooler temperatures in a couple of days.

We also found ourselves hiking through a swampy forest that had mosquitoes and black flies awaiting our arrival. Our only defence was to attempt to outrun them. The problem was that they had wings. It was a losing battle. Score one, for the mosquito-black fly team.

I spoke with Scooby, and he was planning on a short hike of thirteen miles tomorrow. He'd taken a zero today and yesterday to allow his shin splints the opportunity to heal.

DAY 101

LET'S GO SWIMMING
22.8 Miles Hiked; 1,557.5 Miles Total
Start: Mount Wilcox North Shelter; End: October Mountain Shelter

Whistler at the AT Snack Shack.

It was another early start that morning, with big plans for the day. We obviously planned our days around where we wanted to end up, but it's what you can do between point A and point Z that makes for a memorable hike. I really wanted to get to the Upper Goose Pond Cabin that afternoon for a swim, which is a one-hundred-year-old cabin run by the Appalachian Mountain Club. The hot weather made for ideal swimming conditions that I was not going to miss. Train Wreck had indicated that he wasn't interested, so I was going to go alone and then meet up with him later. Well, once we arrived at the side trail to the cabin, he quickly changed his mind. The caretaker, Nancy, couldn't have been more welcoming. We went for a swim and ate our lunch there before moving on to our planned final destination.

Earlier in the day we'd come across a little stand with soda and snacks for sale. This was exactly what I had been talking about and suggesting while on my hike. This person had the entrepreneurial spirit that I'd been looking for. Soda for one dollar; chips and cookies, too—all paid for on the honor system. It was really well done, and so welcome after hiking in the heat. NoBo hikers, turn left on Jerusalem Road, mile marker 1,540.1; the snack shack is about another150 feet down this road and on your right.

We would be hiking through the town of Dalton tomorrow, where mass quantities of food would likely be consumed. We also hoped to meet the Cookie Lady tomorrow.

DAY 102

A PERFECT DAY ON THE AT
22.8 Miles Hiked; 1,578.9 Miles Total
Start: October Mountain Shelter; End: Stealth Camp

Lately, I'd been setting my tent up minus the rain fly. We'd had warmer evenings and no rain, so I'd been taking advantage of the opportunity. Another plus: the open views to the night sky, stars, and full moon. It's almost like cowboy camping, but you are fully enclosed in a screened tent—no bugs.

I didn't start hiking until about six thirty the next morning (I was moving a bit slow). I suggested that Train Wreck go on without me and that I would try to catch up with him later. My first stop was just four miles away: the Cookie Lady's house, a woman who is a legend of the trail, known for baking cookies for hungry hikers. I knew it would be too early to expect cookies from her, but I stopped by just the same.

Lucky, Two-point-oh, and Lioness were tenting on her property, so I chatted with them for a bit and filled up on water from the hose bib. No cookies for Whistler though, so I was back on the trail, headed to the quaint little town of Dalton, Massachusetts.

When I arrived, I bumped into Jukebox whom I had not seen much of for a very long time. I couldn't tell you the first time I had met him, but I recall that it was early one morning when he had just come out of his tent that he had set up on a beautiful cliff/overlook when Scooby and I passed by. Trail named "Jukebox" because he is always listening to his music through ear-buds. We decided to grab lunch together at Angelina's Sub Shop, which has been in business since 1958. The subs were fantastic. Jukebox and I got into a conversation about how close to the end of our hikes we both were. We agreed that anyone who was still hiking at this point was in it for the long haul. In other words, no one who had come that far was quitting. Unfortunately, we'd seen hikers forced to come off the trail due to an injury, which was a reminder that we were all just one step away from being forced off—quite humbling.

Jukebox told me that when he'd first started on March 13, his dad had given him two letters. The first was to be opened at Springer Mountain (I didn't ask about the letter's contents). The second letter was to be opened if Jukebox ever thought about quitting. He informed me that he was looking forward to handing that unopened letter back to his father.

My next stop was the town of Cheshire, Massachusetts for dinner. The trail actually ran right through these towns, which was awesome! Two subs, sodas, and ice cream made for a happy hiker. The temperatures were in the low seventies, as well. To top all that off, I also saw my second bear. This one was huge, but no pictures or claw marks for proof. I heard a huge sound and saw him running away from me—not very graceful at all, either. I could only guess that my hiker body odor had made him run for cover.

I had a friend ask me what a hiker should do if they find themselves hiking with someone with whom they're not compatible? As

I said before, it's difficult to find the perfect hiking companion. One person may be faster or slower than the other, impatient, simply have an overbearing personality, or maybe just isn't a very nice person. This happens in the world of long-distance hiking. One way to separate is to run a bit slow in the morning and suggest they go on, you'll catch up—an effective approach that gives both parties a way out. Try this yourself if you're in such a situation. You'll be glad you did, and you'll definitely enjoy your own hike more.

DAY 103

I THINK I'LL SLEEP IN VERMONT TONIGHT

21 Miles Hiked; 1,599.9 Miles Miles Total
Start: Stealth Camp; End: Seth Warner Shelter

Welcome to Vermont.

What an incredible day it was hiking the AT. I had stealth camped at the base of Mount Greylock last night, and was ready to take it on after my first breakfast of oatmeal and coffee. I stopped in at the Mark Noepel Shelter halfway up for a quick break and my second breakfast of Pop-Tarts.

Mount Greylock is the highest peak in Massachusetts (just under 3,500 feet). I'm not sure what got into me, but I found myself practically running up that mountain. My food bag being almost empty certainly helped.

When I arrived at the summit, I had my third breakfast at the summit lodge of eggs, hash browns, toast, and coffee. Now I was ready for the big descent. I needed to resupply, so I made my way to the Stop and Shop in Williamstown, Massachusetts. It was just a half mile off trail, but as I've mentioned before, miles off the trail always seem longer.

When I arrived at the shopping plaza, I ran into Two-point-oh and Laser Snake at Papa John's Pizza restaurant. They were running a half-price hiker special. Well, okay, then. I never before would have imagined I'd see myself sit down and eat an entire large meat lovers pizza. Hiker hunger is crazy.

I had my resupply shopping completed, and was back on the trail by three that afternoon. I was tenting at Seth Warner Shelter, which was three miles inside the Vermont border. That was now eleven states down, and three more to go.

DAY 104

IT SURE RAINS A LOT IN THE GREEN MOUNTAINS

21.6 Miles Hiked; 1,621.5 Miles Total
Start: Seth Warner Shelter; End: Goddard Shelter

A Feeble Attempt to Dry My Stuff.

It had rained like crazy last night and I was starting to wonder how I was ever going to get on the trail. Luck was with me, though, as there was a break and I was hiking by a quarter past six. The trail conditions started off pretty good, but then the rain started—again. This time there was no stopping. I was soaked to the bone. At first I tried hopping and jumping stone to stone in an attempt to keep my feet somewhat dry. I finally gave up and went stomping through them like my grandson, Brantley would. He would have loved it; me, not so much.

This section of the trail in Vermont is actually part of the Long Trail. The AT follows/shares the Long Trail for 105 of the 273 miles. The Long Trail actually runs all the way to Canada.

I finally gave up and pitched my tent at four thirty that afternoon, crawled in, stripped off my wet clothes, and put on some warm dry clothes. Dinner was fixed, I swallowed it down, and then it was time for very early bed. I could hardly wait to put those wet clothes on in the morning (sarcasm).

DAY 105

I KNOW WHY THEY CALL THEM THE GREEN MOUNTAINS

24.2 Miles Hiked; 1,645.7 Miles Total
Start: Goddard Shelter; End: William Douglas Shelter

Jean, Hugh, and Whistler.

After crawling into my tent last night I was so hungry that I'd actually eaten two dinners. I just couldn't get enough food in me. I was in a constant state of hunger. I was so tired afterwards that I cleaned myself up (as best as possible) and crawled under my quilt. I had slept like the dead that night and ten hours later, it was time to hike again. I couldn't remember the last time I'd ever slept ten hours.

I'd seen bears, lots of deer, turkey, and snakes, and now I'd seen evidence of moose. The "evidence" told me that it was a very large moose. They had the entire mountain range, but they had to use the trail to do their business.

Verizon was fantastic for my entire journey, but it was looking like the service was going to diminish a bit. I was going to continue to write my journal and would upload when service was available.

The green mountain range was lush and—yep—green. If the rain thus far was any indication of normal rain fall, I understood why they called them the Green Mountains. The mud covered much of the trail today. I slipped and fell three times, so you can imagine how filthy I was. It had been over a week since I'd done laundry, so I was going to have to get to a town. A town with a couple of restaurants would be good.

While I was finishing up my first lunch, I met Kazoo and Milly. These very young eighteen-year-old twins had recently graduated high school and decided they would hike the Long Trail. This was their last thing they were going to do together before heading off to separate universities in the fall. I had the pleasure of meeting a lovely couple, Hugh and Jean Joudey, that day, as well. They had been the caretakers of Stratton Mountain Lookout Tower for many years (since 1947). It turned out that Hugh's roots were in Nova Scotia, so they invited me to sit in their cabin to chat. That was fine by me, as they were a lovely couple and I got to get away from the black flies, too.

I spoke with Scooby later that evening, and he was doing great. He'd taken the day off in Dalton to make himself take it easy (and had actually gone to see the recently released movie Wonder Woman). He would hike again tomorrow, but was trying to keep his miles down.

DAY 106

WOKE UP CONFLICTED

5.3 Miles Hiked; 1,651 Miles Total
Start: William Douglas Shelter; End: Manchester, Vermont

The Stillness of a Beaver Pond.

As you'll recall, Scooby had had to take some time to allow his shin splints to heal. I had offered to hang with him through that process, but he wouldn't allow it. His concern was that it could take a long time, or that they might not heal at all. I'd reluctantly moved on, but stayed in contact. Having talked to him last night, it now looked like Scooby was on the mend. I decided to slow down my northerly migration to allow Scooby to catch up, so I pulled a nero, and would take a zero tomorrow. I would hike out on Tuesday, but would keep my miles down. If all went well, he and I would meet up in less than a week.

I hiked a simple 5.3 miles to VT Hwy. 11/30, where I was able to hitch a ride into Manchester. Thank you, Nicki, trail angel, who saw me while heading in the opposite direction, turned around, picked me up, and drove ten miles out of her way to deliver me to McDonald's. While I was there, Crispy came in and we chatted for a bit while we both did some homework. "Crispy" and I had met several times, hiked a bit together and as one of those "twenty something" hikers, he kept a strong pace that would challenge the strongest of hikers.

While eating my Egg McMuffins, I was working the phone to find a place for the evening. I called several hostels but they were all full. One hostel owner I had called gave me a few names and numbers of "locals" that would take in hikers from time to time. After several strike outs I found Terry. Terry picked me up and took me to her home where I was able to shower and do laundry. When I was all cleaned up, I helped out by painting a table for her to show my appreciation. When we were finished with a respectable day's work, we got cleaned up, and went out for dinner.

Some advice for the hikers out there: Stop in Manchester. There are loads of dining and resupply options, and it's a very hiker-friendly community.

Day 107

OH, THE RAIN KEEPS A-COMIN'

0 Miles Hiked; 1,651 Miles Total
Start: Manchester, Vermont; End: Manchester, Vermont

My Reward for Painting Terry's Bathroom.

I spent the night in a real house and slept in a real bed, and was going to again tonight. Terry had most recently placed her name on a list as a trail angel willing to take in thru-hikers. I was her first thru-hiker. I mentioned that I'd painted a table for her, and the next morning I painted her recently renovated bathroom. This was after she'd prepared a terrific breakfast for me. She also prepared dinner as thanks for the work I'd been able to do while I was there. I guess this fell into the category of "work for stay."

After I finished painting, I asked Terry for a ride into town, where I got lunch (McDonald's never tasted so good), coffee at Starbucks (welcome to civilization, Whistler) and caught a movie. I saw *The Mummy* with Tom Cruise (don't waste your time or money). I was going to hike out after breakfast, but it was calling for heavy rain and area flooding of streams and creeks. I was staying with another trail angel tomorrow, though, as Terry's place was not available. I hoped Scooby was better off where he was, but I doubted it. The weather system I was looking at was covering most of the Eastern Seaboard.

DAY 108

I'M SO READY TO MOVE ON

0 Miles Hiked; 1,651 Miles Total
Start: Manchester, Vermont; End: Manchester, Vermont

Princess Poppy Making a Pig of Herself.

The good news was that Scooby was making great progress. We'd spoken earlier and texted later. He was just thirty miles back, so it was possible that we would meet up on Friday—Saturday, at the latest.

The bad news? There was no bad news.

One of my favorite daily stops while I was there in Manchester was Mrs. Murphy's Donuts. It had been my favorite place for afternoon coffee and donuts for the past three days. It's an old time shop that has been recognized as Vermont's best donut shop. Having opened in 1977, they were celebrating their fortieth anniversary that year. It was fun seeing all the old timers sitting around drinking coffee and eating donuts while they solved all the world's problems.

Tonight I would be staying at Jennifer's home, along with a young couple from Montreal. Gabriel and Camille were hiking southbound on the Long Trail, which was helpful for me, a Northbound hiker. I was able to glean a bit of information regarding what was coming up.

Jennifer would drop me off at the trail head in the morning after one more visit to McDonald's for a couple of Egg McMuffins to go.

DAY 109

ANOTHER PICTURE PERFECT DAY

14.8 Miles Hiked; 1,665.8 Miles Total
Start: Manchester, Vermont; End: Lost Pond Shelter

UFO? Nope, a Ski Lift—Minus the Snow.

I was up and about way too early the next morning, but I just couldn't sleep anymore. Jen had set the coffee pot up the night before and had baked a blueberry-walnut coffee cake. I flipped the switch on the Mr. Coffee and cut a slab of coffee cake off that was about as big as the plate I put it on. A couple of hikers had come in late last night, and they now joined me for breakfast as I was having seconds. Goddess and Boss were mother and daughter, and had started their hike where they'd left off last year, at Port Clinton.

Jen was up a bit later, and was ready to drop us off at the trail head. But first we had to make a quick stop at McDonald's for those Egg McMuffins to go, at my stomach's request.

The weather could not have been better. It never got out of the sixties—no rain, part sun, and a nice, stiff breeze that kept most bugs at bay. The trail was actually in really good shape, as well; some mud, but not too bad at all. Today was the Summer Solstice—but it was also "National Hike Naked Day." I would have, but I didn't remember until I was already in my tent for the evening. Apparently, no one else had remembered either (at least none of those hikers I had seen earlier in the day).

There were several really beautiful views (no nudes, just beautiful mountain views). I was really able to take my time and enjoy them. I actually took my pack off and sat down to admire the views a couple of times. I was done with my miles by four that afternoon, and had my tent pitched ten minutes later. Remember, I was trying to do a low number of miles so Scooby could catch up. I was bored beyond comprehension. That only left one thing to do: eat. I had dinner prepared and consumed by six. Then what? There was nothing left to do but hang my food bag and go to bed.

Day 110

I SAY "SUB"; YOU SAY "GRINDER"—TASTES GOOD EITHER WAY

18.6 Miles Hiked; 1,684.4 Miles Total
Start: Lost Pond Shelter; End: Clarendon Shelter

The Rock Garden.

I hadn't intended to hike 18.6 miles the next day. It just seemed to happen.

I got a good, late start in the morning, knowing that I had an easy day ahead of me. I finally started at seven, and really took my time. The elevations and terrain were favorable, too. One of the more interesting sites along the trail was the Rock Gardens of White Cliffs. These stacked stone cairns are said to have been placed there by gnomes. The picture shown above does it little justice, as there are hundreds of these stacked cairns; too many to count and too difficult to clearly show in a photo.

When three o'clock came around, I decided to continue to Route 103, where my AWOL guide described a restaurant called Qu's Whistle Stop. Now in all fairness, Guthook's Guide (AT hiker app) did say that it might be closed. I was willing to take a chance. I hiked the half mile along the 103, and found that it was indeed closed and for sale. I was ready to do an about-face and hike the half mile back, when a car pulled up. I asked if there might be another restaurant close by. I was told there was; Loretta's was just a half mile further up the 103.

Well, as my wife always says, "In for a penny, in for a pound." Onward, I marched. When I arrived, I ordered an Italian "grinder," which is what they call a sub sandwich in that part of the country. It was really a great sandwich, no matter what you want to call it. I followed that up with a Coke, Gatorade, and a pint of ice cream. While I was eating, a gentleman named Uwe sat and chatted with me, and offered to take me the mile back to the trail head. This had definitely been a worthwhile side trip.

Day 111

Less than Five Hundred Miles to Go

14.8 Miles Hiked; 1,699.2 Miles Total
Start: Clarendon Shelter; End: Churchill Scott Shelter

Under Five Hundred Miles to Katahdin.

I wouldn't have gotten up so early, except I'd felt rain in the air. It was supposed to have rained last night, but it had skirted around me, so around five thirty that morning, I just felt like I needed to get moving. My tent was dry and I didn't want to push my luck. I was hiking by a quarter past six, and was in no rush to be anywhere in particular. The rain did find me, though, and did its job well. I was soaked to the bone in no time flat. I didn't even bother to put on my rain jacket, as it was way too hot for that. I just took my lumps and hiked on.

I did have my sights set on the lodge on top of Mount Killington. Mount Killington is the second highest peak in Vermont, and home to an exclusive ski resort. The two-thousand-foot climb to the four-thousand-plus-foot peak was not a very difficult one, but the chair lift is a lot easier, I'm sure. I knew I was hiking a short day because Scooby and I had made our plans to meet on Saturday, so when I made it to the lodge, I ended up spending three hours there. I had a ridiculously over priced meal, as I sat at the bar and enjoyed a local beer while simultaneously taking in the million dollar views. The staff at this very high-end establishment was running around, setting up for a big wedding scheduled for later that evening. I had to laugh to myself when I thought that the mother of the bride might be there, looking at me and wondering when I would leave, or possibly wondering if I was one of the groom's guests. The thought of crashing the wedding did actually occur to me. Although, I might have stood out—especially when I'd ask the bride for a dance.

When I arrived at Churchill Scott Shelter later that evening, I ran into Lilo and Stitch, a wonderful couple who I'd leapfrogged numerous times. They snapped a tent pole while setting up, and were really distraught. Not to worry; Whistler came to the rescue. I had a piece of tubing to repair tent poles that I'd carried with me for 1,700 miles. It had now finally come in handy.

Scooby was just five miles behind me, and was going to meet me at tonight's campsite first thing in the morning. We would then hike five miles to Mountain Meadows Lodge, grab a bite, and make our plans.

I love it when a plan comes together.

DAY 112

THE SCOOBY AND WHISTLER SHOW CONTINUES

5.9 Miles Hiked; 1,705.1 Miles Total
Start: Churchill Scott Shelter; End: Mountain Meadows Lodge

The Bear Meets Princess Poppy.

Yep, I know—Scooby and I hiked a whole 5.9 miles after we met up. I
can explain the reason for this seemingly pathetic day, though. Scooby
met me at the Churchill Scott Shelter at eight thirty the next morning,
as planned, and we hiked the couple of miles to the Inn at Long Trail,
as planned. Both Lucky and Lioness were there, which gave us the opportunity to catch up with one another and tell our tales. "Lucky" was
a terrific young man from Ireland that Scooby and I had hiked with a
number of times and "Lioness" had been hiking with him for a pretty
long time as well (I think another trail romance is being formed...) We
did laundry and waited for the pub to open at eleven thirty, like we'd

planned. From there, we started to make our way to the Mountain Meadows Lodge. We took a slight detour, though.

While on the trail, we met The Bear, who was posting a sign for trail magic. The Bear had had to come off the trail because of a blown-out knee, and decided he would offer an act of kindness instead of continuing on with his hike. Hot dogs and soda pop makes for happy hikers. We spent about an hour there, and we enjoyed hearing his stories, as well.

After our hot dog snack, we made our way to Mountain Meadows Lodge, checked in, showered, and obviously made plans for our next feeding. With pizza on the way, we then finalized our plans for the next few days. It was hard to believe we would be entering New Hampshire later that week (state number thirteen), and the much-anticipated White Mountains. I was really pleased to have my hiking buddy back. It was much more enjoyable to share the experience with someone, especially with a great guy like Scooby.

Day 113

NORTHERN VERMONT, I LOVE YOU

22.2 Miles Hiked; 1,727.3 Miles Total
Start: Mountain Meadows Lodge; End: Stealth Camp

Scooby and Whistler at Thundering Falls.

With breakfast included in our room rate, a late departure was pre-dictable. Cereal, orange juice, coffee, fruit salad, yogurt, and quiche demanded our time and attention. Once our breakfast obligations had been met, we were on the trail by a quarter to eight.

Vermont—or what we dis-affectionately called "Vermud"—was actually kind to us. With the most beautiful clear skies, the mud wasn't bad at all, especially when you considered all the rain we'd had recent-ly. There were a couple of big climbs, but I looked at them as training for what was soon to come in the "Whites." Actually, the entire previ-ous 1,700 miles had been our training for the Whites.

Two notable sites we visited that day included Thundering Falls and later that day, "The Lookout". Thundering Falls is the largest wa-terfall in Vermont on the AT. The Lookout is a privately owned cabin, but can be used by hikers. There is a stair-type ladder that leads to a railed platform on the roof. The views from this platform are priceless. I could have sat up there all day.

Our incentive to move on from the Lookout? Ice cream at On The Edge Farm on Vermont Route 12. Scooby and I polished off a pint each, and washed it down with a cold soda. That was just what the doctor had ordered to help us with our last 2.5 miles of the day. Tomorrow would take us to the town of Norwich, Vermont, where a couple of mail drop boxes awaited me.

DAY 114

A SENTIMENTAL JOURNEY

19.5 Miles Hiked; 1,746.8 Miles Total
Start: Stealth Camp; End: Norwich, Vermont

Celebrating Whistler's Birthday.

The weather the night before was spectacular, with clear skies and a refreshing, mountain-air chill. Stars lit up the sky, which called for a no-rain-fly night for my tent. I laid in my tent staring at the sky above me, and realized that the end of my journey was so very close. While hiking you have that time to reflect on what's happened, what's happening, and what's going to happen. I thought back to when I had first started this dream.

I remember counting the miles hiked each day and adding them to the total. Those were the miles that had brought me closer to achieving this monumental task. I now found that I was subtracting and counting down to how many miles were left before we reached Katahdin. Those were the same miles I had left before I could go home. Home was where Annie was; I hadn't seen her since March 5, that first day at Springer when we'd said our goodbyes. Sure, that all sounds so sentimental, but isn't that all part of the journey? There I was, typing my journal entry on a smart-phone keyboard with one hand, and wiping tears away with the other. Yep, it was all part of the journey—life's journey.

I woke up the next morning, started packing up, and pulled our food bags out of the tree we'd hung them on the night before. As was the routine, I delivered Scooby's bag to his tent. It was one of those pleasures that he always appreciated. He said it was like magic; he woke up, and his food bag was there, waiting on him.

We had hiked for forty five minutes when we came to a creek crossing, and there was a cooler on the other side. Trail magic? There was only one way to find out. I was the first one to cross, as I hung on to the cable strung across to aid with the rapid force of the raised creek. Yes! Soda as trail magic was always welcome—even at seven in the morning. That sugar rush was truly appreciated with the climb we were getting ready to face.

The hike, again, was really kind to us. We had a beautiful walk through a conifer forest, deep-piled pine needles, and limited mud ("Vermud"). Our destination was the town of Norwich, Vermont, where I would be picking up a couple of packages that awaited me. My sister and my son, my daughter-in-law, and my granddaughters had sent Birthday greetings to the hotel where Scooby and I had booked a room. My son Richard, his wife Lauren, and my precious granddaughters sent me a small backpack-size bottle of Irish whiskey that I was going to enjoy on my actual birthday, June 30. The girls had also made homemade birthday cards for Grandpop Whistler.

My sister's method of delivering her gift box to me deserves a mention. Susan is an avid baker when she isn't practising medicine as a family practitioner. Her chosen brand of flour is King Arthur. This storied company has been producing flour since 1790, and is highly regarded in the world of baking. The company also happens to be headquartered in Norwich. Anyway, Susan developed a relationship with Laurie, a customer service representative for King Arthur. Susan shipped my box filled with hiker goodies to Laurie, and Laurie, along with twelve of her friends, delivered it to the Norwich Inn (which is a beautiful property, by the way, and one that I highly recommend). We gathered in the hotel's pub, ate, drank, and of course they sang happy birthday to me. It was an incredible evening, and one that I would not forget.

Tomorrow was another big day. We would be saying farewell to Vermont and would greet the great state of New Hampshire.

Day 115

HELLO, NEW HAMPSHIRE

25.2 Miles Hiked; 1,772 Miles Total
Start: Norwich, Vermont;, End: Smarts Mountain Campsite

Hello, State Number Thirteen: New Hampshire.

We were up and ready to roll early the next morning. We had made our plans last night, which included breakfast in Hanover. Crossing the Connecticut river had us leaving Vermont and entering New Hampshire in our first thirty minutes of hiking.

Once in Hanover, we were kindly directed by a passerby to Lou's restaurant. Lou's must have a history that I'm unaware of, but the free doughnuts for hikers as a starter to my breakfast certainly got my full attention. I ordered the Red Flannel Hash, which is corned beef hash with two poached eggs, potatoes, and toast. It was a perfect start to a perfect start. A problem did rear its ugly head when I discovered one of my trekking poles was missing its tip. This required some "working the smart phone." I had my REI order done while enjoying my last cup of coffee. Unfortunately, I really needed the new poles ASAP, and had to order them via overnight delivery. A hefty mailing fee made the purchase a painful one, but they would be waiting for me to pick them up tomorrow—they had better be.

After we were finished, Scooby and I hit the trail, and it was a bit late because of my trekking pole mishap, knowing that we had to hike twenty-five miles. New Hampshire was proud to give us a small taste of things to come with a few big climbs, too. A threat of late afternoon storms just missed us. We could feel the air changing, see the dark clouds rolling in, and could hear the thunder. The radar on my phone showed the storm band splitting and going around us—how lucky. Our luck did run out, though.

Later in the day, we still had another hour of hiking to get to our planned camp destination when another storm brewed. We were going as quickly as our tired bodies could, but we weren't fast enough. The skies opened up with high winds, rain, and hail just as we reached the top of Smarts Mountain—now that really smarted. We were soaked in no time, and freezing cold. All I could do was put my rain jacket on and wait it out (kind of like closing the barn door after the horses already got out).

When it finally quit, I found a small patch of flat ground between two tents already pitched. Seriously, I pitched my tent within inches of these other tents. It was all I could do, as the space was so limited. Scooby found another site for his tent that was practically directly on the trail...desperate times call for desperate measures. I crawled into my tent, dried off, and put on dry clothes. I wished they were warm clothes, but I wasn't picking those up until tomorrow. My sister Susan had mailed them to the hostel we would be staying at tomorrow. There I was in my tent, shivering, with my winter gear twenty miles further north—misjudged that one by one day. Oops! FYI, winter gear is required once you find yourself entering the White Mountains. Weather can be unpredictable in the White mountains with severe weather conditions including freezing temperatures which can place a hiker in serious danger.

DAY 116

THAT FALL ON SMARTS MOUNTAIN REALLY SMARTS!

20 Miles Hiked; 1,792 Miles Total
Start: Smarts Mountain Campsite; End: Hikers Welcome Hostel

View from Mount Cube.

I'd posted yesterday's journal entry, but what nobody knew was that I'd written it at one thirty in the morning. After getting caught in that rain, sleet, and hail, I was so wet and cold that all I wanted was to get warm and go to sleep. I eventually woke up and wrote and posted my journal, and then went back to sleep. Fast forward to five in the morning, when I rolled over and went back to sleep. Fast forward to six, when I woke up again and realized that I had to get up. It had to be forty degrees, if not colder.

Scooby and I had agreed on a departure time of 7 a.m., so I really needed to get moving. Oatmeal was cooked and eaten, and I enjoyed my coffee while I packed up.

We started down Smarts Mountain and ran into Acorn, whom I had not seen for weeks. I was in the lead, when I came to a boggy spot on the trail. I stepped on what I thought was a secured bog board, but was actually a floating log. I ended up in the bog up to my thighs. Yep, it wasn't pretty. I was covered in mud, and I ended up with a two-inch gash on one leg. I got as clean as I could and hiked on to the next creek, where I was able to clean and dress my wound properly.

A bit later, we had another good climb up Mount Cube. At just 2,900 feet, there are views of almost 360 degrees. This was just a tease for what we would start seeing in the coming days while hiking the White Mountains. We met Huff-and-Puff while we were at the summit of Mount Cube. When we got around to sharing trail names, Huff-and-Puff recognized me, and Scooby by association, because he followed me on Trail Journals.

About five miles later, we met Carl, the Omelette guy. Carl was set up directly on the trail, with a huge canopy tent and outdoor kitchen. This was his second year making omelettes for hikers. He provides trail magic all hiking season long—every day, May through September. He'll make you an omelette or pancakes. He has coffee, juice, muffins, cookies, and bananas. The best part for me was that when I walked up, he recognized me from trailjournals.com, too. He was able to recite everything about my hike. I thanked him for his generosity, and for following me on my journey.

Tomorrow was when we would actually enter the Whites, specifically Mount Moosilauke, which is almost a five-thousand-foot peak.

Day 117

WARM, SAFE, AND DRY

9.2 Miles Hiked; 1,801.2 Miles Total
Start: Hikers Welcome Hostel; End: Kinsman Notch

Scooby and Whistler at the Summit of Mount Moosilauke.

We had agreed to make today a short one for a couple of reasons: First, we knew Mount Moosilauke was going to be a bit of a challenge. At just under five thousand feet, we wanted to get our "feet" wet and take our time. We also knew that bad weather was expected, so we planned accordingly. And finally, we really wanted to enjoy the summit as much as possible.

The climb up was steep and rocky, but with no serious risks. The summit was absolutely breathtaking. At that elevation, you are completely above the tree line, with 360-degree views that make for an awe-inspiring experience. From my perspective, the reward far outweighs the effort of the climb.

The first thing Scooby and I did as we approached the summit was suit up. Rain/wind jackets were needed to provide shields from the intensive high winds, and the rain that was just starting to come down.

The winds would easily knock you over if you didn't brace yourself against it. The cold rain and wind helped guide our decision to start our long descent on what we knew was the steep side of this intimidating mountain. To top things off, the rains intensified to the point that we needed to seek shelter. Fortunately, Beaver Brook Shelter was halfway down, so we made that our destination.

As we arrived at the shelter it really started to pour. Five hikers, McFlurry, Sequoia, Laser Snake, Grizzly, and Lobo, were already in there enjoying what Scooby and I had been seeking: safety and shelter. Now out of the rain, I put on some warm clothes and made myself lunch. I checked the radar on my phone and it didn't look good. It was only two in the afternoon, and it was looking like we were trapped.

An hour later, I saw a break coming on the radar and Scooby agreed with me that we should make a run for it. My thought was that the rocks couldn't get any wetter. It was very slow going, but that was okay if it meant we got there safely. As steep as it had been coming up on the south side, it was twice as steep and difficult on the north side. We took our time, and we were so lucky that the rain held off.

We were stealth camping at Kinsman Notch, where we pitched our tents, ate dinner, hung our food bags, and crawled into our tents just as the rain started coming down hard again. We must have been living right.

I was in my tent, warm, safe, and dry, on the Appalachian Trail. It had been a good day—a very good day.

Day 118

It Keeps Raining on My Parade

11.6 Miles Hiked; 1,812.8 Miles Total
Start: Kinsman Notch; End: Kinsman Pond Campsite

Left Field and Scooby.

The plan was to hike out at six the next morning, but it rained all night and right into the morning. When six o'clock came around, Scooby sent me a text that said his vote was to wait until seven to decide what to do. I texted back and said I was in full agreement. I had no problem rolling over and going back to sleep. Things did start clearing up by seven, so we started packing up, and hit the trail at eight.

Fifteen minutes into our hike, we crossed the Kinsman Notch parking lot, and a car pulled up. A three-time AT hiker, Left Field, jumped out of his car and asked if we were thru-hikers. When we replied with an affirmative, he pulled out a couple of cold beers for us. Sure, it was only eight in the morning, but beer provides lots of nutrients, and is actually considered a breakfast beverage in some countries (I don't know which countries, but I heard this somewhere, I think). Anyway, it was June 30th...my birthday, and I could do whatever I wanted. Left Field did offer us another, but we passed, because we did have mountains to conquer, after all, although we did accept the candy bars he offered. Candy bars are also actually a breakfast food in some countries.

Our hike after that was tough—real tough. The White Mountains truly live up to their reputation. The boulder climbs were tough enough, but throw in all the standing water, ankle-high mud, and raised creek levels that required cautious fording . . . our progress was slow. Very slow. I had two slip and falls, with no physical/bodily harm, but a lot of mud to clean up. The climbs required hand-over-hand at times, and it really tested my physical and mental abilities. There were several times that if not for tree roots to grab on to, I'm not sure how forward progress could have been made. At one point I had been hiking up another very steep ascent and felt my forward momentum come to a complete stop and could feel myself balancing between falling backwards and being suspended in mid step when all of a sudden I felt an ever so slight push from behind. Scooby was right on my heals and saw that I was at the tipping point and gave a me a little nudge to keep me from falling. I was so appreciative of my hiking partners alertness but, it might had been a bit of self preservation as well as I would have fallen on him thus taking us both down. Our low mileage that day was evidence of the slow advance we would make through the Whites. Our goal was to do our best and to stay healthy. The big mile days would just have to wait for when conditions were right.

We camped at the Kinsman Pond Shelter that night, which is run by the Appalachian Mountain Club and a caretaker, with a ten-dollar fee required to tent. This was the first year that the Appalachian Mountain Club was experimenting with giving hikers a 50-percent off card with their first stay at one of the Club-run sites. It was also good for discounts at their huts on snacks and drinks. It sounded like a good deal, so we would see how it worked for us.

Our plan for the next day—if all worked out as planned—was to hike five miles to Franconia Notch, and either hitch a ride or call for a shuttle to Lincoln, where we could resupply, then get back to the trail and add on some more miles. Unfortunately, it looked like rain again tomorrow.

DAY 119

LEFTOVERS NEVER TASTED SO GOOD

7.5 Miles Hiked; 1,820.3 Miles Total
Start: Kinsman Pond Campsite; End: Liberty Springs Campsite

Lonesome Lake.

While I had researched and planned my thru-hike, I had set some personal goals, and had hoped I might enjoy some of those fun and iconic memories that I had read so much about. One of those experiences was now realized.

The Appalachian Mountain Club has full jurisdiction over the huts and campsites. The "huts" are elaborate structures, each with a full dining room, bathrooms, and bunk rooms for paying guests. When I say "paying," I mean *paying*. The rate for a bunk is about $140 per night, per person. This could be costly for a thru-hiker, so we tend to not stay at the huts. They are very popular, however, and with reservations required, they tend to fill up. There are eight of these in the Whites, and they each can accommodate anywhere from forty to a hundred people, depending on the particular hut. Your fee also includes breakfast and dinner.

Back to my goal: The "croo" (sounds like and means "crew," but spelled "croo") will allow thru-hikers to finish off the leftovers if you arrive after any guests and the croo have eaten. Scooby, Grizzly, Lobo, and yours truly did just that.

We arrived at Lonesome Lake Hut at the perfect time. We had cold cinnamon-raisin oatmeal, cold scrambled eggs, blueberry coffee cake, and apple juice for breakfast. The croo couldn't have been nicer or more welcoming. Leftovers never tasted so good!

After breakfast, Scooby and I got back on the trail, with a visit to the town of Lincoln on our agenda for a food resupply. We hiked to Franconia Notch, took a side trail, a distance of 0.9 miles, to the visitors center, and looked for someone who would drive us the 3.5 miles to Lincoln. We were there for about thirty-two seconds before I asked a gentleman if he would take us into town. "Why, of course! Hop in. I'd be happy to," he replied. He got us to the Price Chopper grocery store, but first we wanted to get laundry done. The coin laundry was right next door.

As soon as we walked in, a man walked in after us and asked if we were thru-hikers. We told him we were, and he offered to take us back to the visitors center after we completed our business. We explained that we still had a couple of hours before we would be ready. No problem, he told us. Limping Eagle, trail angel, was awesome for waiting and giving us that lift.

Finally, back on the trail with full stomachs, clean clothes, and full food bags, we started up Mount Lafayette. We were getting a late start, so we set a reasonable goal, which was to get to Liberty Spring Campsite. This would be a good time to mention that our goal was going to require a 2.9-mile, very steep climb up Mount Lafayette—and that we were trying to beat an oncoming severe thunderstorm. We did our best, but we failed. All I can say, is that setting up a tent in rain and high winds was never on my wish-list.

Tomorrow we would climb the rest of Mount Lafayette, which peaks at 5,260 feet. I was hoping for a clear morning so there would be some spectacular views.

I journaled from inside my tent—almost dry, almost warm, but most definitely happy to be on the AT.

DAY 120

HARD MILES DO PAY OFF

17.2 Miles Hiked; 1,837.5 Miles Total
Start: Liberty Springs Campsite; End: Zealand Falls Hut

The Croo at Zealand Falls Hut.

The rain the night before was of biblical proportions. I found that my tent was no longer waterproof, as evidenced by my having had to mop up my tent floor all night. I still got plenty of sleep, though, and Scooby and I were on the trail at a quarter past six, and ready to get some miles in.

Our last couple of days had been pretty unproductive for the rain storms, and to be honest, the Whites were kicking our butts. I'd read how you could pretty much count on reduced miles while hiking through the White Mountains, and I'm here to tell you that that's no lie. It's also psychologically draining to go from hiking twenty-plus miles in a day, to half that amount. You actually start to question if you are physically capable for what lies ahead. If I'd been hiking alone, I would have seriously questioned myself, but the fact that my hiking partner was dealing with the same demons made it easier to accept. We had discussed this at length, and we agreed that we were going to take it easy, try not to get hurt, and take those miles as they came.

Our major climb today was to the summit of Mount Lafayette. It was a tough climb, and unfortunately for us, no payoff in the way of a view. The summit of 5,260 feet was in a fog that morning, which left nothing for us to see except the trail before us. That was okay, though, because the challenge of the climb was rewarding. It was tough, but it was supposed to be. You make that climb and hope for a view, but sometimes you just high-five each other for your efforts, and move on to the next mountain awaiting your arrival.

That next mountain was Mount Garfield. At 4,500 feet, Mount Garfield had a few tricks of its own. A tough climb with no switchbacks, which called for a near vertical climb. The good news was that we received a 360-degree panoramic view above the tree line.

Next on the hit parade was South Twin Mountain, which summits at 4,902 feet. It, too, was a near-vertical climb that at times required hand-over-hand climbing.

One highlight of the day was stopping in at Galehead Hut for lunch. The Appalachian Mountain Club had issued us both a camp card (we paid ten dollars for it) when we'd camped at one of their campsites. A benefit of the card was that you got a free bowl of soup and two baked goods, which we now happily redeemed.

The next very special highlight for me was this: We arrived at Zealand Falls Hut at seven thirty that evening to fill our water bottles before we were going to hike on in hopes of finding a stealth site for our very tired bodies. When we walked in, the croo greeted us and asked if we wanted dinner. Well, of course we did. The general "rule" is that one or two thru-hikers can do a work-for-stay at a hut. Doing a work-for-stay means you do some work around the hut, and in return you get leftovers and can sleep in the hut. This was something I'd been hoping to experience, if for no other reason than to have the memory of it afterwards.

The croo—Kate, Amber, and Jubilee—allowed us to eat first. Dinner was stuffed shells, corn, and a big fat slice of chocolate cake. My job assignment was to clean the stove burners and drip trays. In the end, those hard miles we'd done had paid off.

DAY 121

SOMETIMES, ALL YOU CAN SAY IS WOW

14.2 Miles Hiked; 1,851.7 Miles Total
Start: Zealand Falls Hut; End: Nauman Campsite

Scooby, Windsurfing a Five-Thousand-Foot Summit.

The work-for-stay last night had also allowed hikers/workers to sleep on the dining room floor—a pretty good deal, since it meant not having to pitch your tent or sleep in a shelter with a bunch of people snoring. All guests know, and are reminded, that lights-out and quiet time is at nine thirty. The fact that Scooby and I were laying on the floor on our mats and quilts didn't stop a group of four from using headlamps to continue their card game late into the evening a couple of feet from where we were laying. When I accepted the fact that they had very little regard for anyone but themselves (while also understanding that they were paying guests while I was not), I moved out to the covered porch. It was a beautiful night, with a sky filled with stars and a bright moon. This was my first time "cowboy camping," and it couldn't have been better. Thank you, late night, card-playing people, for making me move outside. It was awesome!

We were up early, packed, and out of the hut by ten after six the next morning. Our first eight miles were fast and easy—the rest of the day was a challenge. Mount Webster was probably one of the most difficult climbs we'd had on the entire trail thus far. We'd get to a section where we would stand at the bottom, unable to see to the top, and wonder how in the world we were supposed to climb it. The answer was, *slowly*—and one step at a time. It was a put-your-trekking-poles-away and start a hand-over-hand climb—challenging and slow, but fun and rewarding. This was also the first time we had site of Mount Washington, with its summit hidden well above the clouds.

Mount Jackson (another four-thousand-foot climb) was just as challenging, with equally beautiful views. We'd achieved what we'd set out to do today, and were camping at Nauman Campsite, which set us up for an early approach to Mount Washington. Mount Washington is a 6,288 summit, and the granddaddy of the Whites. The spectacular summit of Mount Washington was once able to boast holding the record of the highest wind speeds ever recorded (231 miles per hour)... on the planet. On average, hurricane-force wind gusts are observed 110 days a year here. The main structure on the summit was designed and built to withstand wind speeds of three hundred miles per hour while all other structures are chained and anchored to the mountain. The unpredictable weather here can deliver a severe winter storm in the middle of the summer. Since 1849, there have been nearly 150 reported deaths attributed to hypothermia, exhaustion, exposure, falls and just plain poor planning. In addition to the harsh winter conditions one might experience here, rain falls average 96.9 inches per year.

Don't want to hike up there? No problem, you can drive...in fact the visitors center at the summit will sell you a bumper sticker that reads "My car made it to the top of Mt. Washington". Finally, if hiking or driving to the summit is not your thing you can take the cog train. The Mount Washington cog railway has been delivering tourists to the summit since 1869. A fun fact is that it is an AT hiker custom to "Moon" the cog train. I myself am a bit too modest for that business.

In the meantime, it's difficult to begin to describe in words the spectacular views I saw from some of the highest peaks along the Appalachian Trail. It's equally as difficult to get an accurate and true perspective from photos I took, as they simply serve as nothing more than an injustice to the enormity and awe-inspiring beauty. Some days I hiked for hours, got to the summit, and saw nothing more than my feet on the trail and some fog. Other times, I'd hike mile upon mile, hour after hour, summit, and all I could say—all I could come up with—was "wow." What else could I say? The photos were great, but the burning impressions on my brain will always be there, and I'll never forget them. And every time I think of them, I'll simply say to myself, wow!

DAY 122

HAPPY BIRTHDAY, AMERICA

14.9 Miles Hiked; 1,866.6 total
Start: Nauman Campsite; End: Osgood Tentsite

The Summit at Mount Madison.

Could there be a better way to spend the Forth of July than with the father of our country? Well, that's what Scooby and I did—sort of. I was up at a quarter past four the next morning, with a plan to enjoy my coffee that I'd missed out on the morning before.

I'd had a tough day yesterday, with a few stumbles, rolled ankles, and slips, and falls, that I finally attributed to my lack of coffee. I had also been hungry all day, and made a commitment to myself that I wasn't going to let that happen again. Two cups of java, one pack of Pop-Tarts, and two tortillas filled with pre-cooked bacon and mustard—that's how I started the day.

We left the Nauman Campsite right at six that morning and hiked the 6.2 miles to the summit of Mount Washington. The high winds did their very best to knock us over, and every measured step we took was placed with full caution, for fear of getting blown off our feet. In the end, it was a far easier ascent than we'd been led to believe, so we took our time at the summit to take it all in. With the windchill factor, it was twenty-eight degrees, with sustained winds at thirty-five miles per hour and gusts over fifty miles per hour. Our winter gear came in handy, as we were layered up like it was the middle of winter. In other words, it was a very calm day on Mount Washington. Unfortunately, it was also very foggy, and clouds drifted in just to make sure we wouldn't happen to get a view. So foggy in fact that I nearly walked into the weather station that seemed to appear out of no where. Disappointed for the lack of a view? You could say I was somewhat so, but I still enjoyed the climb and made the best of it.

After we grabbed lunch at the summit snack bar we hiked on. We eventually made our way to the Madison Spring Hut, six miles away, for a snack before we would then take on Mount Madison. Mount Madison was an entirely different kettle of fish. At 5,357 feet, Mount Madison mountain is almost completely above the tree line, and is a monster to both climb (it seemed that we would never get to the summit of Madison) and descend.

When we finally made it off Mount Madison, we made a mad dash (as best we could, with our exhausted bodies) to Osgood Tentsite. We arrived at eight thirty that evening, tired and hungry. Tents pitched, water fetched, and hunger satisfied, we crawled (literally) into our tents. It was now ten thirty, and all I could say was Happy Fourth of July America and a very good night.

Day 123

ONE PERSON CAN MAKE ALL THE DIFFERENCE

17.9 Miles Hiked; 1,884.5 total
Start: Osgood Campsite; End: Imp Campsite

Sunset at Imp Campsite.

When we had arrived at the Osgood Tentsite last night, we'd discovered a very poor-looking location, but it was very late and there were no other real options. New Hampshire has very strict rules regarding where you can camp, with heavy fines applied if the rules have been broken. The campsite was very small, with limited tent spaces that were actually on raised platforms. My only choice had been to set up on an already occupied platform that had room for my tent. Well, the folks already in their tent (it was eight thirty at night) were not real happy with me. I tried my best to be as quiet as possible, but I still interrupted them. It happens. Not much can be done. The next morning

I was able to greet them at four thirty when they woke me to get their early start. It happens. Not much can be done.

Since I was up, I fixed myself an early cup of coffee and had my first breakfast. Scooby and I hit the trail at six thirty, with plans to hike the five miles to Pinkman Notch Visitors Center for our second breakfast.

As we were hiking, we came across several SoBo hikers (southbound hikers) and stopped a few minutes to chat. They'd started southbound in Maine the first week of June, and were just now passing us as we headed north. They had information we needed regarding what was ahead for us, and we had information they needed, so we swapped info.

We arrived at the visitors information center three minutes after nine o'clock. It turns out that they stopped serving breakfast at nine. *No exceptions.* Even though they had piles of food they were pulling out of the service case. To top it off, lunch didn't start until nine thirty. Not a problem for us, really, as we had chores to attend to while we waited. When they reopened, we ordered our sandwiches from a great guy. We pointed to all the breakfast items on the table behind him and joked how we could have helped him with the leftovers. Wouldn't you know that he did just that? Our plates were piled up. Sometimes, just one person can make all the difference in a person's day.

Our hike out of Pinkham started with a slow, creeping climb up Wildcat Mountain, which was appropriately named. With several peaks all above four thousand feet, this mountain was a "wildcat." We decided we needed a break, so we made our way to the last hut of the eight in the Appalachian Mountain Club's inventory—Carter Notch Hut—for a snack, which was just a short distance further for two crazy-tired hikers.

Along the way, we met a trail volunteer/trail angel who went by the trail name "Camo." This enthusiastic fella was hiking the trail, hanging his new handmade "way-finding" signs, when he stopped to talk to us. He pulled out some trail magic (Snickers candy bars), and was so positive, so friendly, and so kind at a time when Scooby and I truly needed it. There we were, feeling exhausted and tired, with still so far to go, and Camo had come along. His positive attitude gave us that hidden energy (the Snickers bars helped, too) we needed to finish out our day. Sometimes just one person can make all the difference in a person's day.

We arrived at Imp Campsite at exactly eight o'clock that evening, which had made for another very long day. We stopped by to check in with the caretaker, and met Mandy, who was so kind and welcoming. We felt like we were part of her family. We paid for our sites and walked away, and I thought to myself, sometimes just one person can make all the difference in a person's day—and I'd been lucky enough to have met three of them.

DAY 124

HIKER HUNGER—IT'S A CRAZY THING

8.1 Miles Hiked; 1,892.6 total
Start: Imp Campsite; End: White Mountains Hostel

White Mountains Hostel.

It's kind of funny how fast you can move/hike when you know there's real food and a real bed waiting at the other end. We only had 8.1 miles to White Mountains Hostel, and we did them in under four hours. It sure helped knowing that there were no four-, five-, or six-thousand-foot mountains in the way. As we made our way along this relatively easy portion of the trail, we were reminded of just how close to the finish we were. Someone had taken sticks and arranged them in the shape of the number "three hundred." Scooby said that a SoBo must have arranged them to show they had successfully hiked three hundred miles. That was when it hit us—it could have been a NoBo who'd arranged them to show how many miles were left before Katahdin.

We were seeing more and more SoBo's every day. Most of the ones we spoke with had started the first week of June, which made that week their first-month anniversary. I thought to myself, Lord, please don't let it take me another month to reach Katahdin. Scooby and I had an arbitrary finish date of July 23, but so much depended on the trail, and especially the weather.

Hikers, you want to stay at White Mountains Hostel. When you first arrive, you're required to change into loaner clothes in the dressing room in the garage. From there, you're directed to the shower for a great hot shower. While you're showering, your clothes (all your dirty laundry) are being washed. There's a freezer of ice cream, a soda machine, a hiker's refrigerator, and all-you-can-eat homemade waffles in the morning, and the house is spotless. Shuttles are provided for resupply and restaurants. The hostel is right off the trail head, 0.2 miles, and I highly recommend it.

Once Scooby and I had arrived and showered, we phoned and ordered pizza and cheese bread to share. Since I'd gotten to the hostel, I'd eaten half a large pizza, a half order of cheese bread, a pint of ice cream, a whole rotisserie chicken, a bag of corn chips, a box of ten chocolate Twinkies, four Ding Dongs, a box of Good & Plenty candy, and had had to drink one Coke, two Powerades, three beers, and a cup of coffee—all of that in less than a ten-hour period. Hiker hunger is a crazy thing.

DAY 125

THAT POOR LITTLE PIGGY

11.8 Miles Hiked; 1,904.4 total
Start: White Mountains Hostel; End: Gentian Pond Shelter

Gentian Pond.

I'd gotten a great night's sleep last night, and I woke up at my usual time. I made myself go back to sleep, as waking at five in the morning doesn't work well when you're at a hostel. When six thirty came around, I woke to the smell of coffee and the all-you-can-eat waffles freshly out of the waffle iron. Four—four was all I could eat. They were huge, crisp, and delicious, but I could only eat four. We were packed and ready to hit the trail at eight thirty—yep, a late start for us.

I believed that I had broken my little toe. I'd been walking through the kitchen in my hostel-issued flip flops when I ran my right foot into a brick fireplace hearth. I wanted to scream out, but I managed to just limp away. A couple of hours later, my small toe was puffed up and had turned black. The only thing I could do was tape it to his buddy next door, take ibuprofen and Tylenol, and hike on.

That made for some tough and slow hiking for me. That was one reason why we decided to quit for the day after just 11.8 miles. The other reason was that we were trying to strategically plan our approach to Mahoosuc Notch, which is thought to be the most difficult and/or "fun" mile of the entire AT. Mahoosuc Notch is a huge, mile-long pit of nothing but boulders in various sizes—some, the size of cars—which makes boulder-hopping the only way to get through. I had also read that because of its location and lack of sun exposure, snow and ice can sometimes be found in the Notch as well. There's never a dull moment when hiking the trail.

We were camping tonight at the Gentian Pond Campsite Shelter. As indicated by the name, there is a pond, and the pond has beavers—lots of beavers, as well—and the pond happens to be our water source. Our obvious concern was proper treatment of the water. I chose to filter and boil mine. Scooby filtered, treated chemically, and boiled his water. The good news? The privy was close by.

Day 126

The Final Stretch

12.2 Miles Hiked; 1,916.6 total
Start: Gentian Pond Campsite Shelter; End: Bull Branch Campsite

Scooby and Whistler at the Maine Border.

We set off the next morning at a quarter past six, knowing that we had an enormously exciting day ahead of us. For one thing, we would cross the New Hampshire-Maine border just six miles into our day.

As we arrived, we were just getting ready to take a few pictures with the sign when a couple of SoBo's arrived, as well. There we were, all excited about Maine being our last state, while this terrific couple was excited to have completed Maine, their first state. Toad and Birdie were newly married, and hiking the AT for their honeymoon. I took their picture at the border sign, and they took a picture of Scooby and me.

The next exciting adventure of the day was the challenge of Mahoosuc Notch, known as that most difficult mile of the trail—and yes, the most fun. It was certainly challenging, that's for sure, but we had to get there first.

The climbs were average, but rain was imminent. We also knew we wanted to take our lunch break before getting to the Notch to get some rest before tackling it. Full Goose Shelter would be the ideal spot, so off we marched. The clouds began to darken, and we could just feel the rain in the air. Distant thunder rumbled, and we just knew it was time to break out the rain gear. The sky split open and spilled a torrential rain down upon us. It wasn't the fact that *we* were so wet, it was that the Notch was now going to be, as well. Difficult enough on a dry day, those boulders would now be wet and slippery.

To top things off, I fell into a bog while attempting a jump across it. I ended up with one leg on a big board, the other in the bog—past my knee. It took all I had to recover myself. I was stuck big time. The bog and I fought like crazy. We both wanted the shoe on my left foot, and I wasn't leaving without it.

I won in the end, but did I ever need a bath. My buddy Scooby had had free entertainment for the day. I think I would have laughed just as hard had the shoe been on the other foot—his, that is.

Once at the shelter, we ate, rested, and talked to some SoBo's about the Notch, since they had just come through it. It was now time for us to hike the last 1.5 miles there.

When we arrived at the Notch, we folded our trekking poles up and stowed them in our packs. This one-mile stretch, a boulder field, required concentration and extreme caution. You literally climb over, around, and under boulders the size of cars, buses, and trains. The Notch is so isolated, the sun doesn't reach it. It's also really cold in spots, so cold that there is still snow and ice down there. Scooby tried to make a snowball, but it was too hard-packed, and more like ice. I took a fall that had me land on my back, but thanks to my backpack, no harm was done, except that the outer elastic pocket on the pack got torn. The solution? I took my knife and cut it off. It took us right at two full hours to make it through that one mile. It was exhilarating and rewarding to complete that section, to say the least.

We were now camped at a stealth site known as Bull Branch, where we would get rest to prepare for a major climb in the morning: Mahoosuc Notch's brother, called Mahoosuc Arm, which is a 1,500-foot climb in just over one mile. Very steep, but fun!

DAY 127

SO FAR, SO GOOD IN MAINE

17.6 Miles Hiked; 1,934.2 Miles Total
Start: Bull Branch Campsite; End: Stealth Camp

Trail Magic from NoBo Joe.

I was well rested when I woke at four the next morning. I made a few edits to my journal first, and then grabbed our food bags from the tree we'd hung them on the night before. The first business at hand was to make my cup of joe. I absolutely loved my early morning coffee while sitting in my tent. There was something about it that just seemed normal when compared to the rest of my crazy day.

Scooby and I were ready and on the trail at a quarter past six, knowing that our early morning hike was going to start with the Mahoosuc Arm climb. I set a pace that got us through it in good time, but it was honestly not as bad as we had heard or read. It might be that it hadn't seemed so bad because of our "fresh" legs, or perhaps it was that cup of coffee or those cherry-frosted Pop-Tarts that made it feel easy.

While coming down Old Speck toward Grafton Notch, some Sunday morning day hikers told us of someone doing trail magic at the parking lot. That got our attention, especially once they mentioned doughnuts and coffee. We started to run down the mountain, with high hopes of getting in on that action.

When we arrived, we met NoBo Joe at his car, which was loaded with beautiful, scrumptious trail magic. NoBo Joe had just finished his thru-hike on July 2, and wanted to pay forward all the trail magic he had received. It was a real special treat that meant so much to us thru-hikers. Thank you, NoBo Joe!

So far Maine had been a beautiful state with really good trail conditions. We'd achieved the mileage we had today because of those conditions and fairly reasonable elevations. You never knew what to expect from the trail. What I did know, was that tonight I was camping next to a brook with the cleanest, clearest, and coolest water you could ever imagine. Plus, who doesn't sleep better when they're next to the sounds of a babbling brook? So far, so good in Maine.

DAY 128

THE HONEYMOON IS OVER

14.6 Miles Hiked; 1,948.8 Miles Total
Start: Stealth Camp; End: Stealth Camp

Tight Sleeping Quarters.

We had such grand plans for the day, but as it turned out, Maine had other plans. I guess our entry the day before into the final state in our journey had been a facade. I'm kidding, okay? Thru-hiking is supposed to be difficult; otherwise, you can just go for a walk down the sidewalk. We really had had a couple difficult climbs, though, that just plain wore us out. We climbed up big mountains and then we climbed down big mountains. Pretty uneventful to be honest. We didn't see a single NoBo, but did see seven or eight SoBo's.

That was all right, tomorrow was another day, and another day of hiking would get us closer to Katahdin—and most importantly, closer to home.

Our grand plan had been to hike eighteen miles, but we quit at 14.6 miles when we found a tentsite. We found what could be considered a "campsite," and made camp at five thirty. The site was so small we could just barely fit both tents. That was okay, though, because all we wanted to do was sleep.

DAY 129

THE LORD PROVIDES AGAIN

17.2 Miles Hiked; 1,966 Miles Total
Start: Stealth Camp; End: Little Swift River Pond

Whistler and Scooby with Snowman, Trail Angel.

Wow, had I ever gotten a good night's sleep. I'd slept from seven o'clock the night before till four thirty the next morning, and was energized for the day. I had actually gotten up to the sound of rain at three, and was concerned that it might have been a soaker coming our way. It ended up being a light rain, which ended quickly, and I went right back to sleep.

When Scooby and I had left Gorham and the White Mountains Hostel four days ago, our plan had been to hitch a ride yesterday into the town of Andover to do another short resupply that would take us the additional two days into Rangeley. We'd discussed changing our plan to go directly to Rangeley, which meant we would have to stretch our current food supplies an additional two days. It could be done, but it was going to be close, and to be honest, we would be hungry—real hungry. However, we both signed up for the plan, and hiked toward this common goal. My food bag was so low and light that I could give you the exact inventory of what was in it. It was hardly enough for the average person, and certainly not enough for a hungry hiker. I was going to have a half-lunch and half-dinner to make it work.

Well, don't you know, that as we were hiking north, three NoBo's we knew were slack packing south for the day, and they told me that Snowman, trail angel, was at the bottom of Bemis Mountain, waiting for me and Scooby, with trail magic. It turned out that Snowman followed trailjournals.com, and had been following my journal. We ran down that mountain, and when we got to the bottom, there he was with a grill fired up and ready to go—hamburgers, hotdogs, sodas, chips, and bananas.

There we were, thinking about how hungry we were and how little food we had left, and along had come Snowman. What a blessing! Snowman had been providing trail magic for some time now, and tried to get to the trail head once or twice each week during hiking season. He kept up with Trail Journals to see who to expect on those days. Well, today had been our lucky day. Thank you, Snowman! It's kind of crazy, but this kind of thing happens to hikers all the time. In a time of need, the Lord (through his trail angels) *does* provide. Amen!

TRAIL ANGEL

I made my choice; it's all on me.
You followed along; I did not see.
I hike each day and do my best,
While you work before me and never rest.
It's always when I least expect,
You show yourself and earn respect.

You do not owe me a single thing,
But here you are, with the joy you bring.
I know not how to ever thank you
For how you give and for what you do.
You give me hope, faith, and love,
For you're the trail angel sent from above.

(July, 11th, 2017, Day 129)

DAY 130

POSSIBLE WITH A LITTLE HELP FROM OUR FAMILY

4.8 Miles Hiked; 1,970.8 Miles Total
Start: Little Swift River Pond; End: The Farmhouse Inn

Pearl and Whistler Playing at the Farmhouse Inn.

The next morning, we had just 4.8 miles to Maine Route 4, where we would walk the 0.3 miles (there is a difference between walking 0.3 miles and hiking that same distance) to the Hiker Hut to pick up our mail drops. I know I can speak for both myself and Scooby when I praise the support we got from our families. My wife and I live in Nova Scotia, which unfortunately for me, made it logistically difficult for my wife to support my hike by way of mail drops as Canada Post deliveries are not always reliable and tough to schedule. A thru-hikers mail drops really are a lifeline and it is imperative that they are at the predetermined address according to that hikers schedule.

Fortunately for me, my daughter-in-law Lauren lives in South Carolina, and she was my lifeline, mailing me my drop boxes with Priority Mail being very reliable (if it fits, it ships...). Trail angel Lauren is the mother of my beautiful granddaughters, works as a pediatrician, volunteers her time at church, runs her household, and made time to help me. I was also blessed to have my sister Susan's help and support. Susan is a family doctor, wife, runs her household, which included having recently moved to a new home that required renovations and a lot of her time. She, too, had found time to help make my journey easier and more manageable. I've said it before, and I'll say it again: How blessed was I?

Scooby had his wife Kellee, who he counted on for support, and she never let him down. His drop boxes were always at the pre-established location, and his needs were always met. The support we got is imperative to a successful thru-hike, and so greatly appreciated.

After we picked up our boxes, we caught a shuttle to our hostel, the Farmhouse Inn. Stacy and her staff ran this two-hundred-plus-year-old farmhouse that is off-the-charts charming. Stacy was beyond accommodating, especially with shuttles to town for meals (including an ice-cream run).

Once we had checked in, we were shown to our room, where we were able to get showered and then we were off to do our laundry.

I've explained what a nero is before, but let me cover it again. A nero is a day to recharge, regroup, resupply, and reorganize for the miles that lie ahead. It's an opportunity to chat with other hikers, too, but at the end of the day, it's still a work day—a work day with very few miles to show for it, but so very necessary.

Our plan was to take the six thirty shuttle the next morning back to the trail head, and hopefully get in fifteen miles over some tough climbs, including Saddleback Mountain and The Horn. But of course, there were thunderstorm warnings for tomorrow. At least I was warm, safe, and dry tonight.

DAY 131

IT WAS A WET AND COLD ONE TODAY

18.7 Miles Hiked; 1,989.5 Miles Total
Start: The Farmhouse Inn; End: Spaulding Mountain Lean-to

Whistler Clowning around in the Town of Rangeley.

The Farmhouse Inn provided everything we needed for a respite from the trail. But all good things must come to an end.

The next morning, Scooby and I were up at five, and agreed that the rain was not going to stop our forward motion. The weather report was calling for rain all day, but we both really wanted to get home. The other fifteen to twenty hikers there were planning on taking a zero for the day, but Scooby, myself, and Crispy were ready to go at six thirty when Stacy agreed to drive us back to the trail head. "Crispy" had become a true friend over the many miles we had hiked together. He has a mild demeanour, is easy to talk with and is one of today's youth that gives you complete confidence in the future. He had ended up at the

Farmhouse Inn with us the evening before and his hiking out with us on this morning was welcomed.

It was ugly outside, but we had mountains to climb. With it being cold and wet, the only solution was to work up some body heat. Saddleback Mountain was pretty tough, especially the exposed ridge that was fogged in and freezing. The rocky surface was wet and slippery, so we moved cautiously, but still made good time. I wanted to take some pictures of the heavy fog, but that would have required me to stop—and I wasn't about to do that. We were up and over the Horn and Saddleback Jr. as quickly as we could.

When I finally had to stop to put gloves on, I realized we'd lost Crispy along the way. We did catch up with him later at Poplar Ridge Lean-to, where we stopped for a quick lunch break. When I say "quick," I mean *quick*. It was way too cold for wet hikers to sit around. We were shivering and had to get moving again.

The rain finally broke while we were doing our last eight miles to Spaulding Mountain Lean-to. Once there, we all fixed dinner and made for our tents to try to warm up.

Tomorrow was going to be a big milestone day for us. We were going to pass the two-thousand-mile mark, and would also get to the less-than-two-hundred-miles-to-go mark. We'd talked about it over dinner the night before, and all of us were in a state of disbelief.

DAY 132

THAT'S TWO THOUSAND MILES DOWN

18.6 Miles Hiked; 2,008.1 Miles Total
Start: Spaulding Mountain Lean-to; End: Horns Pond Lean-to

Princess Poppy Loved This Mushroom.

We were off to the races (on the trail) at six thirty the next morning. It would be the last full day of climbing the Bigelow Mountain Range in Maine. Tomorrow we would have right at eight miles of climbs, and then things would level off for us for a while.

A couple of the day's climbs were pretty intense, starting with a steep climb up and then back down Spaulding Mountain. South Crocker before lunch, and then North Crocker immediately following lunch, which kept the blood flowing. The best part of the day, though, was when we passed the two-thousand-mile mark. We now had under two hundred miles to go.

When Scooby and I got to the two-thousand-mile mark (according to our GPS on Guthook), we formed the number "2,000" out of sticks, and took a few pictures in celebration. Speaking of pictures, the photo on the previous page is of Princess Poppy and some of the wild mushrooms we saw along the way. I mentioned Princess Poppy before, but as a reminder, she belonged to my granddaughters. I took pictures throughout the journey, and sent them along to help keep my granddaughters engaged and a part of my hike. Princess Poppy had been a terrific travel companion, especially because she didn't weigh that much.

With the pictures taken care of, we still had six miles to go for the day, with four of those miles being real steep while thunderstorms lurked. The thunder would roll along as it shook the entire mountain under our feet. It was time to move, and to move up that mountain as fast as we could, or risk a soaking. I'm not sure where the energy comes from after a long day of hiking, but you reach down and grab it and you just go. We won that race fair and square, too.

We made it to the campsite and pitched our tents with a couple minutes to spare before the rain. With dinner in its rightful place (my stomach), I spent a bit of time looking at the miles that remained. I was in my tent, planning the end of my hike, and I was in a state of disbelief. Weather permitting, we would summit Mount Katahdin on July 25. In the meantime, I was going to do my best to enjoy the rest of the journey.

DAY 133

THE RAIN IN MAINE IS A PAIN

17.9 Miles Hiked; 2,026 Miles Total
Start: Horns Pond Lean-to; End: West Carry Pond Lean-to

The Second-to-Last Four-Thousand-Foot Climb.

When Scooby and I had arrived at the Horns Pond Lean-to last night, Crispy had already arrived and was sitting in his tent. He let us know that he had injured his Achilles heal while stepping on a root. This is the type of injury that can end a thru-hiker's hike. I'd been hiking with and leapfrogging Crispy for almost 1,500 miles, and it was upsetting to see something like that happen to someone who had worked so hard.

Scooby and I had had a number of conversations about how each of us was just one step away from a hike-ending injury. It was for that reason that we found ourselves being extremely cautious. Risks that I had taken earlier in my hike were ones I wouldn't consider taking at this point. Those steep descents were very time consuming, as we carefully and slowly planned each foot placement. I'd fallen so many times since the start that I'd lost count. I'd been fortunate, in that each of my landings had allowed me to get up, take inventory, wipe myself off, and continue on. I had cuts, abrasions, and bruises, I'd lost four toenails, I was hiking with a broken toe, and I had aches and pains in most joints. I would wake up in the morning and it would take me a few steps to warm up for a day of hiking. The one thing that kept me going was that I wasn't alone. Everyone out there was in the same boat. My hiking now, especially so close to the end, was all about self-preservation and being able to hike another day.

Today's hike had brought with it the end of the four-thousand-plus climbs. That morning, we'd summited Bigelow Mountain West Peak, at 4,145 feet, and quickly followed it with Avery Peak, at 4,090 feet. Sure, there would be some more climbs ahead, which I called "minors," and of course, there was still the big daddy, Mount Katahdin. It was nice to know though, that the day-after-day major climbs were over. Why was that so nice to know, you ask? Because I was tired!

And what kind of day would it have been if it hadn't rained? It had come down on us hard that day. We tried to beat it, but it was to no avail. We went from cautiously trying to keep our feet dry to sloshing through the mud and puddles, because as I've said before, in the end, it just didn't matter anymore.

Maine had been such a beautiful state so far, so beautiful that I would have to say it was the most beautiful of the fourteen states the AT goes through. It's as though they saved the best for last. Sure, it had its challenges, like lots of mud, rocks, and roots (just ask Crispy), but it also had beautiful scenery, huge and numerous lakes and ponds, and deep, beautiful forests.

I failed to mention the black flies and mosquitoes, however. Let me put it this way: DEET is a product I would never have put on myself prior to being Maine. The label clearly dissuades most people from even considering its use. One warning is that it will melt plastic. But for the sake of my sanity, I sprayed that poison all over my body—sometimes twice a day—because it works. They will still fly around you in an effort to drive you crazy, but they will not land on you. I guess I'll find out the long-term affects one day, but for now I was not feeding the masses with my blood.

DAY 134

CROSSING THE KENNEBEC

19.8 Miles Hiked; 2,045.8 Miles Total
Start: West Carry Pond Lean-to; End: Pleasant Pond Lean-to

How We Crossed the Kennebec River.

We made our way early the next morning, knowing that we'd planned for a big-miles day. Our primary objective was to get to the town of Caratunk to pick up our drop boxes.

I mentioned before how beautiful Maine was. Well, we spent the better part of the day hiking along the shoreline of ponds, cascading waterfalls, rivers, and rushing creeks. East Carry Pond Beach is a beautiful spot with a sandy beach. Had we had the time, I would have loved to have gone for a swim, but we didn't, and to be honest, I'm regretting that decision now. We did stop to take a quick morning break on the rocks overlooking a breathtakingly beautiful pond that will forever be imprinted in my mind.

While walking the trail, which happened to hug the shoreline, we found wild blueberries to our left and to the right. Unfortunately for us, they were not yet ripe. There were so many waterfalls, ponds, and streams, that if time had allowed it, we could have lingered all day.

So why didn't we? Well, we were on a strict timeline. We had to get to the Kennebec River before two o'clock that afternoon, and we had fourteen miles to hike to get there in time. The Kennebec River is four hundred feet wide, and too deep and too unpredictable to ford. It's a hydroelectric dammed river with gates that can be opened unbeknownst to a hiker trying to cross. The Appalachian Trail Conservancy operates a free ferry service from nine in the morning to two in the afternoon, and we knew we needed to hustle there or we would have to wait till the next morning.

The ferry, by the way, is a canoe with a white blaze painted on the deck. As a hiker, you stand on the shore and wave at the attendant, and he gets in his canoe, paddles over, and takes two passengers at a time. One of the two has to paddle. That was my job.

Once we were on the other side, we called the Sterling (a hostel where our mail drops had been delivered to) from the free phone at the post office for a shuttle. Caratunk is a small, sleepy town with no cell service. We got picked up and got our boxes, and then had lunch prior to heading back to the trail by four that afternoon for the last six miles of the day.

When we got to the campsite, we pitched our tents just in time before our daily rain. You can never have enough rain, you know. Gosh, if it hadn't rained, then the mud and ankle-high standing water on the trail might have dried up. We couldn't possibly have had that. If that were to have happened, what would I have slipped and fallen in? Nope, that would never have worked. That's why it had to rain every day. That was okay, though. I still loved it!

DAY 135

OF BLUEBERRIES, POND SWIMS, AND NIGHT HIKES

24.3 Miles Hiked; 2,070.1 Miles Total
Start: Pleasant Pond Lean-to; End: Stealth Camp

Wild Maine Blueberries.

It wasn't a real big climb, but Pleasant Pond Mountain got us warmed up early the next morning. At just under 2,500 feet, it also provided the height we needed to make a few phone calls. I called my wife, as I hadn't had service for a couple days. While I was doing that, Scooby called his wife, as well. He then contacted Shaw's Hiker Hostel in Monson to make our reservation for tomorrow night. I made a quick call to talk with a friend who would be picking us up after our summit on July 25. I just couldn't believe it!

Now that that business had been taken care of, it was time to lay down some miles. While crossing under a series of power lines, I noticed some ripe blueberries. Yep, I had to sit for a moment and eat a small handful. I got to check "eat wild blueberries while hiking through Maine" off the list.

The next thing I knew, we found ourselves hiking along Moxie Pond. Don't you know, there was a dock with a ladder. Incentive for a swim? Check "swim in a pond while hiking through Maine" off the list. Scooby was not all that interested in swimming, so we agreed to meet up later. I just knew I would have regrets if I hadn't gone for that swim in that beautiful pond.

After a delightful swim in water that was just so cool, clean, clear, and refreshing (which made it difficult to get out), I got back to my hike. I tried catching up with Scooby, to no avail. It was starting to get late, and I was too tired and hungry to continue. He would be just a mile or two ahead of me, so I'd catch up in the morning or simply meet him at Shaw's Hiker Hostel. I found the perfect site, and made camp at a stealth site along a cascading river. It was just spectacular.

I'd eaten my dinner and gotten myself cleaned up (a ritual involving wet wipes each evening), when all of a sudden I heard a person call out. It was an ATC ridgerunner, wanting to speak with me at eight o'clock in the evening. I got myself dressed and crawled out of my tent. There was the "law," waiting on me. I was too close to a water source, and she told me I had to move. Too close to a water source was pretty funny, as you couldn't walk ten feet in Maine without being too close to a pond, river, stream, or brook. Well, she insisted that I pack up and move. I explained that I was really tired after a long day of hiking. She let me know that I should have planned my hike better. Hmmm, how had I ever made it from Georgia to Maine? A freak accident, I suppose. Message received, loud and clear!

I wasn't all that happy, but I obliged. Besides, I needed to hurry, because there were another five hikers camped south of me on the river that she would need to wake up and have move before her shift was over. I got re-dressed, packed everything up (while she watched over me), put on my headlamp, thanked her for the advice about planning better when I hiked, and hiked another two miles in the dark woods of Maine. I found a perfect spot right at the edge of the one-hundred-foot-wide, knee-deep stream I was going to ford in the morning. Yep, I was too close to a water source. Check "night hike in the dark woods of Maine" off the list.

I was pretty excited about tomorrow, because dear friends were meeting me in Monson with trail magic. Shelby was a master in the kitchen, and she and her husband Al were going to meet Scooby and me at lunchtime. Today had been a good day, and tomorrow was going to be a good day. Every day was a good day!

DAY 136

ALL IS GOOD WITH THE (MY) WORLD

6.7 Miles Hiked; 2,076.8 Miles Total
Start: Stealth Camp; End: Shaw's Hiker Hostel

Whistler and Grey Beard Meet.

When all was said and done, I still got a good night's sleep. Yes, I broke a rule and camped within seventy five feet of a water source, and for that, I deeply apologize . . . but rushing water helps me sleep.

Monson was calling my name, and I forded the stream so fast that my feet were almost dry (that's an exaggeration). While I was wringing out my socks on the north side of the creek, it started raining (of course). It was a light rain, though, so it was of the slow-soaking variety. The terrain made for quick hiking, so I didn't bother to put on my rain gear, as it was also warm, which would translate into *hot* with a rain jacket on. What happened next will require me to give some backstory.

My sister/trail angel, Susan, had shared a story about an eighty-two-year-old man she knew from Tennessee. Dale Sanders is a hyper-athlete who still competed in a variety of sports activities. He happened to be thru-hiking the AT, and if he completed it he would be the oldest male to do so. Susan had recently let me know that he'd "flipped" to Katahdin to start southbound that past week. Dale knew that Baxter State Park would close up mid-October if early winter weather conditions dictated and he didn't want to chance not being able to summit. Susan knew Dale (trail name, "Greybeard") personally, and asked me to keep an eye out for him and take a picture with him.

As I was hiking that morning, and within a half mile of Maine Route 15 where I was going to get picked up, I saw an old fellow hiking toward me, and I just knew it was Greybeard. He wasn't alone, and he was apparently rarely alone due to his notoriety. Firefly was hiking with him, and had a smile from ear to ear on her face. As I approached, I introduced myself as Whistler, which didn't mean anything to him. But once I mentioned my sister Susan, he started jumping up and down and clapping his hands. What a neat gentleman! God bless you, Dale "Greybeard" Sanders.

When I arrived at Maine Route 15, I called Shaw's Hiker Hostel and asked for a shuttle just as their shuttle happened to be pulling up to drop off hikers. Perfect timing! Once at the hostel, all was good with the (my) world.

The best part of my day involved my dear friends I mentioned, who would be coming to Shaw's to bring us trail magic. Well, Al and Shelby arrived around eleven with a couple of coolers and grocery bags full of her delights: breaded chicken cutlets, a couple pounds of her famous pimiento cheese (it's a Southern thing), whoopie pies, two different types of fresh-baked brownies, potato salad, chips, soda, and all the fixings. Lunch was absolutely amazing. Guess what was for dinner?

I can't express my appreciation enough for these two special friends. They drove 250 miles round-trip to provide all of that incredible trail magic.

Tomorrow was another big day for us, as we would enter what's known as the "Hundred-Mile Wilderness." This section of the trail is extremely remote, and one of the most exciting parts of the trail. Why is it so exciting, you ask? Well, because after we exited the Hundred-Mile Wilderness, we would have just seventeen miles left of our journey. All was good with the (my) world.

DAY 137

ENTERING THE HUNDRED-MILE WILDERNESS

21.6 Miles Hiked, 2,098.4 Miles Total
Start: Shaw's Hiker Hostel; End: Stealth Camp

Entering the Hundred-Mile Wilderness.

Monson was a great stop to take a nero before entering the hundred-mile wilderness. Shaw's Hiker Hostel was one of the best hostels we'd stayed in along the two-thousand-mile journey. One of the options at Shaw's was their nine-dollar breakfast. Three eggs, bacon, hash brown potatoes, coffee, juice, and all the blueberry pancakes you could eat. I needed to get back to the trail just to work off that breakfast.

Scooby and I had made a decision. I mentioned my desire to go for a swim two days ago, and how pleased I was that I'd taken the time to enjoy it. This served as a reminder that the end of our journey was fast approaching. It also made us both realize that we had to be certain there would be no regrets. Scooby and I had hiked well over one thousand miles together, and had enjoyed the companionship of each other over the course of all those miles. These final one hundred miles are traditionally a time for thru-hikers to reflect back on their hike; we agreed the only true way to do that was to hike alone. We had made a commitment to each other to take those final days for ourselves, but to summit Mount Katahdin together on the twenty-fifth of July.

When the shuttle dropped me off that morning, it became abundantly clear that I was only 115 miles from completing my thru-hike. It was difficult to believe that I would be home one week from now. I won't say I was sad, because I wasn't. I was excited! I couldn't wait to summit Katahdin, but I was really excited about the prospect of going home—home to see Annie, home to see friends and family, home to share all about my adventure, and home to hear about how life had gone on in my absence.

First I had to get there, and the only way was to keep on hiking, so I didn't fool around. Even though I'd gotten a late start (dropped off at a quarter to nine), I cranked out 20.6 miles. I was hoping to get an early start tomorrow and chip away at those remaining miles.

The trail itself wasn't too challenging that day—or should I say, not as challenging as the SoBo's had made it sound. I'd come to realize that when you asked a SoBo a question about the trail they'd hiked, they really had nothing to compare it to, so I would listen to what they said, but not take it too seriously. Tomorrow I would hike the "chair backs," which was a number of up and down climbs.

DAY 138

WE'RE FINISHED REFLECTING

20.6 Miles Hiked; 2,119 Miles Total
Start: Stealth Camp; End: Logan Brook Lean-to

Mount Katahdin as Seen from Whitecap Mountain.

The next day was a tough one, to say the least; lots of "uppa-downs" that just beat me up. I'd started just before six thirty that morning, and had a big up right out of the gate. I'm not making this name up: Chairback Fourth Mountain just seemed to have gotten the best of me, and it never really got much better.

I think there was a combination of factors that contributed to my poor hiking. First of all, I was tired of climbing mountains. It seemed the closer I got to Katahdin, the less I wanted to make those climbs. The only mountain I was the least bit interested in climbing was Katahdin. The other contributing factor was that I wasn't hiking with my hiking buddy. This time to reflect was for the birds. Time went by so slowly without having someone to talk to.

Three peaks were particularly difficult. West Peak, Hay Mountain, and Whitecap Mountain are each over three thousand feet, and come one after the other. To top things off, it was pretty hot, and I ran out of water at the peak of Whitecap. The only redeeming factor was that I got to see Mount Katahdin for the first time when I reached the summit of Whitecap.

The lean-to I was hoping to camp at that night had a perfect tentsite for me, right next to the babbling brook. Yes, I wasn't seventy-five feet from the water, but designated campsites must be an exception to the rule.

I arrived, got water first (I drank a liter in about ten seconds), and then pitched my tent and made my dinner. About an hour later, who showed up? Yep, that's right. Scooby arrived, looking just as dejected as I had. He got water, pitched his tent, and started his dinner. That's when he told me he was finished reflecting on his hike, and asked if we could hike out together in the morning. He'd said the same thing I had thought—it just wasn't the same. We had hiked too many miles together to not finish it off that way.

Tomorrow would hopefully be a better day. In addition to now being back together as a duo, the elevations were really going to level out.

DAY 139

THIS PLACE IS GOING TO THE DOGS

27.4 Miles Hiked; 2,146.4 Miles Total
Start: Logan Brook Lean-to; End: Nahmakanta Campsite

I could almost feel the pull of that great mountain. It seemed that I couldn't move my legs fast enough to get myself to the prize.

The next day, we averaged over three miles per hour, up until noon, when we had already hiked 14.7 miles. The terrain and elevations certainly helped, as it was relatively flat with limited roots, rocks, and bogs. In fact, it hadn't rained for a couple of days, so a dry trail hiked best.

One of the day's highlights came a short time after we'd left Logan Brook Lean-to. I had heard from a friend to be on the lookout for a dalmatian on the trail—not a real one, but one made of concrete, like the ones you might see in front of a firehouse. Well, we found it perched up high on a boulder and looking down on us as we were about to pass it. I figured that there had to be a way up, so I climbed up for a photo op.

The "lowlight" of the day was when we walked into a nest of yellow jackets. We must have looked like a couple of clowns trying to outrun a swarm of those stinging insects.

The rest of the day was all about putting down miles and getting through the hundred-mile-wilderness. It was fun though, when a SoBo would pass and ask if we were NoBo thru-hikers. I couldn't help but get this wide grin on my face and simply say, "Yes, yes, we are!"

Scooby and I got to our planned campsite at about six that evening, and collected water, pitched tents, made dinner, and literally crawled into our tents. Our feet were killing us, and our bodies needed as much rest as we could give them. Tomorrow was another big day—big because it would bring us closer to Mount Katahdin, and ever closer to home.

DAY 140

THE SOUNDS OF SILENCE

21 Miles Hiked; 2,167.4 Miles Total
Start: Nahamkanta Stream Campsite; End: Rainbow Lake

Rainbow Lake.

I guess there really was a time and need for reflection. You just couldn't force it. It just had to happen all on its own.

I was up at four thirty the next morning, and couldn't sleep, so I started my morning routine. First off, was the private stuff, and then I was off to pull down our food bags. I always dropped Scooby's off at the vestibule of his tent, and could usually hear him still sawing logs. I made my first cup of coffee and ate my breakfast to the sweet sounds of silence.

Once we were both ready to go, we agreed that there was no sense in killing ourselves, and that we would take it easy. Scooby and I then started our hike at the usual time of six thirty.

One great thing about our relationship was that we could—and did—talk about just anything. But that day, it was a bit different. There seemed to be long periods of dead silence. It had become painfully obvious to me what was happening.

I finally stopped dead in my tracks, and with tears running down my face, turned and choked out, "Why is this so"—blanking—"difficult?" Except I didn't say blanking. Unsurprisingly to me, Scooby had those same tears running down his face. He knew I wasn't speaking to the difficulty of our hike, but that I meant the difficulty of knowing it was coming to a conclusion. We were both privately reflecting while we hiked, and we were both dealing with what we knew was coming. What was coming nearer and nearer, and coming faster than we realized, was the end of our journey. We both joked and said that neither one of us had been crying; we'd just gotten black flies in our eyes. So we marched on.

A short time later, I had a thought, and without stopping or looking back, I suggested to Scooby that he should lead the way up Mount Katahdin that coming Tuesday. He responded that we'd done just fine with me leading and him following. Still with my back turned, I told him that I wanted that to be my gift to him, that I wanted him to see that sign at the summit of Katahdin first. I could hear him choking, and through his cracking voice, he agreed. I didn't look back or say anything else, because there was nothing else to be said.

So we marched on to the sounds of silence.

A bit later, we found a lakeside beach to have our morning break. There were wild blueberries that we picked and enjoyed, but the best part was not being rushed. We just sat, looking over the beautiful lake, and again, enjoyed the sounds of silence.

Later in the afternoon, we stopped at a stream to filter water, and decided we would eat lunch there. Again, not rushed, we enjoyed our lunch, then laid back and watched the clouds drift by. How often do grown men lay on their backs and watch clouds go by? Not often enough.

Later that night, we were camped on Rainbow Lake. Our tents ended up about fifty yards apart, for the minimal sites in the pristine wilderness. I was in my tent after enjoying and finishing off most of what had been left in my food bag. Tomorrow we would hike eight miles to Abol Bridge, where we would stop in at the Baxter State Park Ranger Station to register for our summit on Tuesday (weather permitting).

As I wrote in my journal, I listened to the wind blow through the tall pines, the waves lapping the lakeshore, and a loon that was giving its relentless call. The sounds of silence were beautiful.

DAY 141

BIGGER FISH TO FRY

17.7 Miles Hiked; 2,185.1 Miles Total
Start: Rainbow Lake; End: The Birches

Mount Katahdin as Seen from Abol Bridge.
5.3 Miles to the Summit of Katahdin

The hundred-mile wilderness was a bit of a challenge, but not as much as we'd been led to believe, and besides, we knew we had bigger fish to fry—Mount Katahdin.

Our original plan had always had a bit of wiggle room in it, and it looked like it was going to work in our favor. We'd built an additional day into the plan in case we had bad weather. Mount Katahdin is an unforgiving, formidable mountain, and a summit on a wet and rainy day can be hazardous. Granite can get slick when wet, and those boulder scrambles are not real fun if you slip. To top things off, Scooby and I were wearing trail runners that, to be honest, had seen way too many miles. Both pairs had blown-out sides, worn-and-thin treads, and soles that were starting to separate. It was okay, though, because we had duct tape, medical tape, and KT tape with us.

Our original plan had been to hike eight miles to Abol Bridge and camp there for the night. We would have hiked in the additional ten miles the next day to register our stay at the Birches, which was at the base of Katahdin, and then hike the remaining 5.3 miles to the summit on Tuesday. Well, it turned out that tomorrow (Monday) was calling for clear skies, while Tuesday was calling for heavy rain. We decided to summit according to the forecast.

We went the additional distance to the Birches and registered for our summit, which would happen the next morning. I was in my tent, just 5.3 miles from the summit of the tallest mountain in Maine: Mount Katahdin. Normally, I would share the highlights from our hike that day, but to be honest, what else is there to say? Did I mention that I was just 5.3 miles from the summit of Maine's tallest mountain, Mount Katahdin?

The climb tomorrow would be a steep one, for sure. We were starting at six thirty in the morning, and believed it would take us between four and five hours to climb, and almost as long to come back down. I would be eating a big breakfast (two packs of Pop-Tarts instead of one) to get me fueled up.

It is beyond impossible to describe this mountain in words. It reminds me of the time I visited the Grand Canyon, and later, people would ask me to describe it. You can't! When we saw Katahdin from Abol Bridge, we'd been ten miles away from it. It was so massive and seemed close enough to touch, yet it was still ten miles away. The next pictures I would take would be from its summit, which for the record, is at 5,267 feet. I was going to touch that sign with my bare hands.

I can't begin to describe my angst, my excitement, or my emotions, but I will attempt to later at the journey's conclusion. My hope is to fully capture the event in a meaningful way that serves it justice. But in the end, it's just a mountain. Anyone can come to Baxter State Park and take an entire day and climb it (well, maybe not just anyone), but we hiked 2,189.8 miles to have that honor and privilege. How blessed was I?

I would soon attempt to put into words in my journal what it was like to complete the most time-consuming and, to be very honest, selfish adventure I could have ever imagined.

DAY 142

SUMMIT DAY

5.3 Miles Hiked; 2,190.4 Miles Total
Start: The Birches; End: Mount Katahdin

The End.

I couldn't sleep for all the tea in China. It wasn't so much about it being the big day tomorrow, but more about that cup of coffee I thought I'd needed after dinner. What had I been thinking? I used the time I couldn't sleep wisely, though. I looked at the seven-hundred-plus pictures I had taken over the last four and a half months. I was so restless that my legs were shaking. I probably should have put on my hiking shoes, backpack, and headlamp and hiked Katahdin. I think it must have been around midnight when I finally got to sleep.

Four thirty came early (not really any earlier the normal, but it just felt like it had). I was up and rolling, with no time to waste. I had that mountain to climb. Scooby and I were on our way by 6:20, and we were juiced. As we'd previously discussed, he led the way. This was difficult for me, and felt different, but I managed. He was on fire, and pulling me into the flames with him. The decision to summit a day early had taken the planned short day for rest out of the equation, but it had absolutely been the right decision. The weather could not have been better; a little overcast, but cool, and there was no chance it would rain.

All of our decisions were being made in a bubble, though, as we had no way of communicating with friends or family, for the zero amount of cell coverage at Baxter State Park. My friend, who was picking us up from Baxter, had made his plans for the twenty-fifth. My wife had made plans to meet him in Halifax to take me the rest of the way home, as well. We would deal with all that business once we'd reached the summit, where we would have our emotional breakdowns first, and then work the phones from the summit, where we were told we could get a signal.

The climb up the mountain was fun, and the walk up to the falls was an easy, casual walk. From the falls on to the summit, though, it got tough. One particular section, at the point just above the tree line, is where you stow your trekking poles and make a near-vertical, hand-over-hand climb—so appropriate, and lots of fun, to say the least, for our last big climb.

We made it to the summit and sign right at ten that morning, after just 3.5 hours of hiking. It was difficult for me to be able to express myself with regard to how I felt. I was definitely thrilled, and couldn't wait to touch the sign, but as I said earlier, I had already done a great deal of reflection and shed a good number of healthy tears. It seemed that I was more concerned about taking those all-important pictures and calling my wife, than anything else. Perhaps it hadn't really hit home yet. Maybe sometime next week it would fall on me when I least expected it.

I really don't know what else to say. Don't misunderstand me; it's not like it was a letdown. It's just that it was a well-planned and expected event that, when finished, I accepted the fact that it was time to go home. Would I feel the same tomorrow? Next week? Or next month? I had no freaking idea! All I did know, was that I wouldn't be lacing my hiking shoes tomorrow, because I was done. I was going home.

Gordon (the friend from Nova Scotia and an '03 thru-hiker) was going to meet us for breakfast at the Appalachian Trail Cafe at five the next morning. From there, we would drop Scooby off at the Bangor Airport, where he would pick up a car for his fourteen-hour drive back to his wife Kellee, and his home in Cleveland, Ohio. Then it was off to Nova Scotia for Whistler, where Annie would meet Gordon and me in Halifax to drive me the rest of the way home. I was going to be sleeping in my bed tomorrow night!

GOODBYE, DEAR FRIEND

As this journey comes to its end,
It's time to say goodbye dear friend.
The days have gone so quickly by,
my steps too quick the reason why?
To take it slow as some may go,
Were they right, I do not know.
Did I do all that I could,
or regrets for what I should?
I woke up daily with a goal,
To give my all, my heart and soul.
My body hurts, my muscles ache,
It's alright though, that's what it takes.
I know in time my body will heal,
the hurt forgotten, the memories real.
It's been a gift I believe.
But was I worthy to receive?
The day has come to no longer roam,
It's time my friend that I go home.

(JULY, 24TH, 2017, DAY 142—THE END OF THE JOURNEY)

Well, there you have it. That was my journey. It's mine and I own it! My thru-hike can never be taken away from me. This event was without a doubt the most difficult thing I have ever done, but at the same time, the most rewarding. When Scooby and I were close to the end of our hike, we asked each other if we would ever hike another long trail. Without hesitation, we both responded with a big fat *no*. We both agreed—been there, done that.

Well, time has passed and my body has healed, and I currently find myself planning my next hike. The Pacific Crest Trail has been calling my name. Will Scooby hike again with Whistler? He didn't say yes—but he didn't say no, either. Stay tuned!

EPILOGUE

Whistler's Walk was nothing less than a dream come true. Without sounding too melodramatic, it was life changing for me. My perspective on all things important and unimportant took on new meaning. I find that I am more patient today, more understanding and accepting, as well. I took on a monumental task that was without a doubt the most selfish thing I had ever done, while my wife Annie did the most selfless thing I could have ever imagined: She let me go for a long walk—a 142-day walk.

I learned something very important that I want to share with you, the readers of my book. Our future looks bright and we are going to be okay. Today's youth and tomorrow's leaders are smart, strong, and tough. I spent 142 days hiking with members of a younger generation I felt honored to have met, and am proud of beyond my wildest dreams. God bless our young people!

I believe there are several unanswered topics that require closure now:

Dale "Greybeard" Sanders did complete his thru-hike, and is now in the record books as the oldest person to have completed the Appalachian Trail.

Crispy recovered from his injury and completed his thru-hike as well.

My total mileage in this book is recorded as having been 2,190.4, but the official distance of the trail in 2017 is 2,189.1 miles. Why the difference? I posted my miles according to the GPS app called Guthook, which can account for some of the differences in mileage. The only thing I can say about that is no matter what the correct mileage was, I hiked every mile of it!

I gave credit and thanks throughout my adventure to my family and trail angels but, I want to use this opportunity to give a call-out to Gordon "Gimp" Warnica. As one of the class of 2003 thru-hikers, he was an invaluable resource in preparation for my hike, one of my trail angels, as well, drove from Nova Scotia to Baxter State Park to give Scooby a ride to a rental car agency, and me a ride home.

Yes, I'm currently planning my next hike for 2019: the Pacific Crest Trail. A second book in the Whistler Walk series? That remains to be seen.

Scooby and Whistler received the green light for Trail Days 2018 from our wives—the blessings continue.

Lastly, I would like to offer my sincere thanks and appreciation to Steve, Michael, Jennifer, and especially my editor, Lindsay, of Palmetto Publishing Company for their patience and high level of professionalism.

About the Author

Now retired after a successful thirty-one-year career, Bill Monk, an American-Canadian, currently lives in Nova Scotia with his wife of thirty-eight years, Ann Marie. They own and operate A Seafaring Maiden Bed and Breakfast, Ann Marie's 140-year-old ancestral home in Granville Ferry, Nova Scotia. An outdoor enthusiast, Bill enjoys hiking, kayaking, snowshoeing, and biking, and his hobbies include furniture restoration, woodworking, and the loving care and maintenance of their historic heritage home.

72452653R00170

Made in the USA
Middletown, DE
05 May 2018